MEAT

C·O·O·K·B·O·O·K

GOLDEN APPLE PUBLISHERS

MEAT COOKBOOK

A GOLDEN APPLE PUBLICATION/
PUBLISHED BY ARRANGEMENT WITH OTTENHEIMER PUBLISHERS INC

JUNE 1986

GOLDEN APPLE IS A TRADEMARK OF GOLDEN APPLE PUBLISHERS

ISBN 0-553-19849-1

Contents

Beef

Barbecued Beef Steak on a Bun

1½ to 2 pounds beef top round steak, ¾ to 1-inch thick
2 tablespoons flour
2½ teaspoons salt
⅛ teaspoon pepper
2 tablespoons cooking fat
1 small onion, finely chopped
½ cup water
¼ cup brown sugar, firmly packed
2 tablespoons prepared mustard
¼ teaspoon celery salt
Dash of ground cloves
1 (6-ounce) can tomato paste
¼ cup cider vinegar
1½ teaspoons Worcestershire sauce
Few drops of hot pepper sauce
1 small green pepper, cut into strips
6 Kaiser rolls or 8 hamburger buns, split

Partially freeze steak; cut into strips 1/8 inch thick and 2 to 3 inches long.

Combine flour, 1 teaspoon salt, and pepper. Dredge strips; brown in fat in large frying pan. Pour off drippings. Add onion and water to strips; cover tightly. Cook slowly 30 minutes.

Combine brown sugar, mustard, 1-1/2 teaspoons salt, celery salt, and cloves; sprinkle over strips. Stir in tomato paste, vinegar, Worcestershire sauce, and hot pepper sauce. Cook, covered, 20 minutes; stir occasionally. Add green pepper; cook 10 minutes. Serve on rolls. Makes 6 to 8 servings.

Braised Beef with Vegetables

1	red pepper	4	slices round steak, each
1	green pepper		approximately 4 ounces
1	small Spanish onion	½	teaspoon salt
2	medium-sized tomatoes	⅛	teaspoon pepper
2	medium-sized zucchini	⅛	teaspoon dried basil
2	tablespoons vegetable oil	½	cup white wine

Cut peppers in half. Remove seeds; slice into thin strips. Slice onion. Peel tomatoes; cut into eighths. Clean zucchini; cut into 1/2-inch-thick slices. Heat oil in large frying pan or Dutch oven. Add all vegetables; cook about 10 minutes, stirring occasionally.

Trim fat from steak.

Lightly grease ovenproof casserole; place 1/3 of vegetable mixture in dish. Arrange steak on top. Sprinkle with salt, pepper, and basil. Cover with rest of vegetables. Pour wine over vegetables; cover casserole. Cook in preheated 350°F oven 50 minutes. Ten minutes before end of cooking time, remove cover to reduce liquid. Makes 4 servings.

Sweet-and-Sour Brisket

1	(5- to 6-pound) brisket	1	cup catsup
2	onions, sliced	1	cup water
1	clove garlic, minced	1	tablespoon salt
¾	cup brown sugar		Ground pepper to taste
½	cup vinegar		

Place brisket on onions and garlic.

Mix other ingredients; pour over brisket. Cover; roast in 350°F oven until tender, approximately 4 hours. Makes 10 to 12 servings.

Boiled Corned Beef

1 (3- to 5-pound corned-beef round)

Place corned beef in Dutch oven or heavy pan; cover with cold water. Bring slowly to boil. Simmer, covered, 3-1/2 to 5 hours or until tender. Remove from broth; let stand 15 minutes before slicing.

Cabbage wedges and potatoes can be cooked in broth for old-fashioned corned beef and cabbage. Makes 4 to 6 servings.

Chili Beef with Vegetables

Chili Beef with Vegetables

1½ **pounds beef chuck, cubed**	12 **small onions, peeled**
2 **tablespoons flour**	2 **carrots, sliced**
Salt and pepper	1 **parsnip or 1 turnip, sliced**
1 **level teaspoon chili**	1 **pound potatoes, sliced**
powder or to taste	2 **cups stock or water and**
2 **tablespoons oil**	**beef stock cubes**

Season flour with salt and pepper and chili powder. Coat meat in flour. Heat oil in a saucepan and fry meat until browned. Add onions, carrots, parsnip or turnip, potatoes, and stock. Bring to a boil, stirring occasionally.

Pour mixture into a baking dish and cook in a 325°F oven for 2 hours or until the meat and vegetables are tender. Makes 4 to 6 servings.

Chipped Beef Deluxe

2 tablespoons fat or oil	½ cup water
½ cup celery, chopped	1 (4-ounce) package dried beef
2 tablespoons green pepper, chopped	
2 tablespoons onion, chopped	2 tablespoons pimiento, chopped
1 (10½-ounce) can condensed cream of mushroom soup	2 hard-cooked eggs, diced
	3 cups cooked noodles (about 6 ounces uncooked)

Heat fat. Add raw vegetables; cook until they begin to brown. Stir soup, water, and beef into vegetables. Cook, stirring as needed, until thickened. Add pimiento and eggs. Serve on noodles. Makes 6 servings.

Note: In place of mushroom soup and water, you can use 2 cups milk and 1/4 cup flour. Gradually blend milk into flour.

Cranberry Pot Roast

3 to 4 pounds beef arm pot roast, cut 2 inches thick	3 tablespoons prepared horseradish
2 tablespoons cooking fat, if needed	6 medium-sized carrots, cut in 2-inch pieces
2 teaspoons salt	6 small onions, cut in half lengthwise
¼ teaspoon pepper	
4 whole cloves	½ cup cranberry sauce (whole-berry)
1 stick cinnamon	
½ cup water	2 tablespoons flour

Brown meat in own fat (trimmed from meat) or in cooking fat, if needed, in large frying pan. Pour off drippings. Sprinkle salt and pepper over meat. Add cloves and cinnamon.

Combine water and horseradish; add to meat. Cover tightly; cook slowly 2-1/2 hours. Turn meat.

Add carrots and onions to meat. Cook, covered, 40 minutes or until meat and vegetables are tender. Remove meat and vegetables to warm platter.

Blend cranberry sauce with flour; combine with cooking liquid. Cook, stirring constantly, until thickened. Reduce heat; cook 3 minutes. Makes 6 to 8 servings.

Note: For beef blade roast, reduce initial cooking time 30 to 45 minutes.

Corned Beef and Onion Hash

1 **tablespoon oil**	3 **level tablespoons catsup**
2 **onions, sliced**	**Pinch of mixed dried herbs**
1 **(7-ounce) can corned beef, chopped**	1 **(2½-ounce) package instant potato**
1 **cup or small can baked beans**	**Salt and pepper**
	Chopped parsley

Heat oil in large frying pan, add onion, and fry until tender. Chop corned beef finely and add it to onions with baked beans, catsup, and herbs.

Make up potato as directed on side of package and stir it into ingredients in frying pan. (Cold leftover mashed potatoes can be used—about 1 cup.) Add salt and pepper according to taste. Serve garnished with chopped parsley. Makes 4 servings.

Corned Beef and Onion Hash

Spicy Pot Roast

1 **(3- to 4-pound) rolled rump roat**	1 **teaspoon ground cumin**
½ **cup flour**	1 **teaspoon salt**
2 **tablespoons cooking oil**	½ **teaspoon pepper**
1 **cup onion, chopped**	1 **(8-ounce) can tomato sauce**
2 **cloves garlic, minced**	½ **cup water**
1 **teaspoon beef bouillon granules**	½ **cup cold water**
1 **teaspoon celery seed**	**Hot cooked rice**

Coat roast on all sides with 1/4 cup flour. Brown on all sides in Dutch oven or heavy casserole in hot oil. Add onion, garlic, beef bouillon granules, celery seed, cumin, salt, pepper, tomato sauce, and 1/2 cup water. Cover with tight-fitting lid. Cook over low heat until tender, 3 to 3-1/2 hours. Remove meat; keep warm.

Measure pan juices; add water, if necessary, to make 2-1/2 cups.

Blend together 1/4 cup flour and 1/2 cup cold water; stir into pan juices. Cook and stir until bubbly and smooth. Strain over sliced meat and rice. Makes 8 servings.

Marinated Beef Roast

1 **clove garlic, minced**	1 **(4-pound) rolled rump roast**
1 **teaspoon ground black pepper**	3 **tablespoons olive oil**
1 **bay leaf**	2 **tablespoons flour**
1½ **cups dry red wine**	2 **tablespoons water**
2 **tablespoons lemon juice**	

Combine garlic, pepper, bay leaf, wine, and lemon juice in enamel pan or deep glass casserole. Add roast; turn several times to coat with mixture. Cover; let marinate in refrigerator at least 24 hours; turn occasionally.

Heat oil over moderate heat. Remove roast from marinade; pat dry. Brown on all sides in hot oil.

Meanwhile, preheat oven to 375°F.

Pour marinade over roast in Dutch oven; cover tightly. Place in oven; cook 2 hours. Uncover; bake 30 minutes. Transfer pan to stove; remove meat to warm platter.

Make a paste with flour and water; thicken pan gravy. Slice roast. Serve with gravy and oven-fried potato wedges or boiled or mashed potatoes. Makes 8 to 10 servings.

Beef Pastry Roll

Beef Pastry Roll

½ cup self-rising flour
¼ level teaspoon cayenne
    pepper
2   tablespoons margarine
Milk to mix
1   cup cooked beef, diced
1   strip bacon, finely
    chopped

1   level teaspoon prepared
    mustard
2   tablespoons catsup
Salt and pepper
Pinch of dried thyme
1   level teaspoon parsley,
    chopped
Tomato sauce for serving

Sift flour and cayenne pepper into a mixing bowl. Rub in margarine with the fingertips until mixture resembles fine bread crumbs. Add enough milk to make a soft dough. Knead lightly, then roll out to an oblong 1/8 to 1/4 inch thick on a lightly floured surface.

Put all remaining ingredients into a mixing bowl and stir until combined. Spread meat mixture on the dough and roll up. Cut into 1-1/2 inch slices and place them on a lightly greased baking sheet. Bake in a 400°F oven for 20 minutes or until golden. Serve with tomato sauce. Makes 4 servings.

Beef in Red Wine

3 to 4 pounds boneless beef (rump, sirloin tip, or round)
½ teaspoon salt
¼ teaspoon freshly ground black pepper

Marinade
3 cups red wine
1 cup water
½ cup onion, sliced
¼ cup carrots, sliced
1 clove garlic, minced
1 bay leaf, crumbled
2 teaspoons fresh parsley, chopped
1 teaspoon thyme

Braising Ingredients
2 tablespoons vegetable oil
2 strips lean bacon, cubed

1 ounce brandy, warmed
1 veal or beef knuckle
1 tomato, peeled and quartered
1 tablespoon fresh parsley, chopped
1 bay leaf
3 green onions, chopped
1 cup beef bouillon
½ teaspoon salt

Vegetables
10 small white onions, peeled
8 carrots, peeled and shaped like small balls

Parsley for garnish
2 tablespoons flour
2 tablespoons butter
3 tablespoons Madeira
2 tablespoons cognac

Rub beef with salt; sprinkle with pepper. Blend all marinade ingredients. Pour marinade into glass or ceramic bowl. Add beef; turn it several times, so that all sides are coated with marinade. Cover; marinate in refrigerator 12 to 24 hours. Turn beef occasionally. Remove beef from marinade, drain. Pat dry with paper towels. Strain; reserve marinade.

Heat oil in large Dutch oven. Add bacon; cook until transparent. Add beef; brown well on all sides. Drain off fat. Pour warm brandy over meat. Ignite; wait until flames die down. Add remaining braising ingredients; cover pan. Place in preheated 350°F oven. During cooking, occasionally pour some reserved marinade over beef. Cook meat 3 hours.

Meanwhile, prepare vegetables. Add onions and carrots to Dutch oven; braise 1 hour. When meat and vegetables are tender, remove from oven; place on preheated platter. Surround with onions and carrots. Garnish with parsley. Keep food warm.

Strain sauce through fine sieve. Skim off fat, if necessary. Cream together flour and butter. Thicken pan sauce with all or part of this. Stir and heat to boiling 1 to 2 minutes. Add Madeira and cognac. Adjust seasonings.

Spoon some sauce over meat; serve rest separately. Makes 6 servings.

Roast Rump of Beef

Roast Rump of Beef

1	**(3-pound) rump roast**
1	**pound potatoes**
1	**pound parsnips or pumpkin**

Salt
4 **tablespoons drippings or lard**

Wipe meat all over with a clean, damp cloth. Peel potatoes and parsnips or pumpkin, cut into pieces, and parboil in boiling salted water for 10 minutes. Drain well.

Put drippings or lard in the roasting pan and put it in 350°F oven until hot. Add vegetables and stir so that all pieces are coated in fat. Put meat in center of pan and arrange vegetables around it. Baste meat with some fat, then roast in 350°F oven for 20 minutes per pound plus 20 minutes over. Makes 6 servings.

Roast Beef au Jus and Yorkshire Pudding

1 cup all-purpose flour	4 pounds rolled rib roast
¾ teaspoon salt	2 pounds potatoes
2 large eggs	1 cup stock
1 cup milk	½ cup fresh horseradish, grated
1 cup shortening for roasting	

Prepare pudding batter: Sift flour into mixing bowl. Add salt; make hollow in center. Add eggs and a little milk. Stir and draw flour into center gradually until smooth. Add remaining milk; beat well. Let stand 30 minutes.

Melt shortening in roasting pan. Place roast (thawed, if frozen) in pan; baste well. Roast in preheated 450°F oven 15 minutes per pound; baste every 15 minutes.

Peel potatoes; boil 5 minutes. Drain; scratch with fork to make crisp. After 15 minutes put in pan with meat; cook about 45 minutes.

After 30 minutes, pour off about 1 tablespoon fat drippings from meat into small, open pan; reheat. Add Yorkshire pudding batter; place at top of oven until well risen and brown, about 30 minutes.

When roast is cooked, place on heated platter with potatoes and Yorkshire pudding; keep warm. Pour off all clear fat; make gravy with juices in roasting pan, adding stock. Stir and scrape well to loosen all meaty brown bits. Season to taste; strain.

Serve with grated horseradish. Makes 8 servings.

Beef Round over Noodles

2 tablespoons peanut or corn oil	1½ pounds beef round, cut into 1-inch pieces
1 teaspoon soy sauce	1 tablespoon Worcestershire sauce
½ teaspoon sugar	1 teaspoon garlic salt or 1 clove garlic, minced
2 teaspoons sherry	1 can mushrooms (optional)
3 cups onions, thinly sliced	
2 teaspoons cornstarch	
1 tablespoon soy sauce	

Heat oil in large skillet with 1 teaspoon soy sauce, sugar, and 1 teaspoon sherry. Sauté onions.

Mix cornstarch, 1 tablespoon soy sauce, and 1 teaspoon sherry in bowl. Dredge meat in mixture; coat every piece. Put meat in onion mixture; brown. Stir in Worcestershire sauce and garlic salt. Cover skillet; let simmer 1 hour adding mushrooms, if desired, for last 10 minutes; stir occasionally.

Serve on bed of noodles. Makes 4 to 6 servings.

Sauerbraten with Gingersnap Gravy

1 (4-pound) beef rump roast	½ cup cider vinegar
2 onions, thinly sliced	¼ cup vegetable oil
8 peppercorns	½ teaspoon salt
4 cloves	2 cups boiling water
1 bay leaf	10 gingersnaps, crushed
1 cup mild white vinegar	½ cup sour cream
1 cup water	1 tablespoon flour

Place beef in deep ceramic or glass bowl. Add onions, peppercorns, cloves, and bay leaf. Pour white vinegar, water, and cider vinegar over meat. Chill, covered, 4 days. Turn meat twice each day.

Remove meat from marinade; dry well with paper towels. Strain marinade into bowl. Reserve onions and 1 cup marinade.

In Dutch oven, brown meat on all sides in hot oil. Sprinkle with salt. Pour boiling water around meat. Sprinkle in gingersnaps; simmer, covered, 1-1/2 hours. Turn often. Add 1 cup reserved marinade; cook 2 hours or more, until tender. Remove meat; keep warm. Strain cooking juices into large saucepan.

Mix sour cream with flour in small bowl. Stir into cooking juices. Cook, stirring, until sauce is thickened and smooth.

Slice meat into 1/4-inch slices; add to hot gravy. Arrange meat on heated platter; pour extra sauce over. Makes 8 to 10 servings.

Exotic Steak

Steak Diane

3	well-marbled strip sirloin steaks, cut ½ inch thick	1	tablespoon parsley, freshly chopped
2	tablespoons butter	1	(10½-ounce) can beef consommé, chilled
2	tablespoons cooking oil		Salt and pepper to taste
2	tablespoons brandy	1	teaspoon Worcestershire sauce
2	tablespoons shallots or green onions, minced		

Pound steaks with mallet or wine bottle to 1/4 inch thick. Pierce steaks with tines of fork on 1 end; roll up steaks. Unroll 1 steak into sizzling butter and oil in heavy skillet. Cook 1 minute on each side. Remove to heated platter.

Place remaining steaks, 1 at a time, in hot-oil mixture; cook 1 minute on each side. Return steaks on platter to skillet. Turn heat to high; pour brandy over steaks. Ignite brandy; shake pan until flame is extinguished. Reduce heat; cook 1 minute. Add shallots; cook 2 minutes. Sprinkle with parsley, stirring well. Add consommé, 1 spoonful at a time, to steak mixture in skillet; bring to boil. Spoon about 2 tablespoons pan liquid onto warm platter. Remove steaks to platter; keep warm.

Cook pan liquid vigorously until reduced by half. Season with salt and pepper; stir in Worcestershire sauce. Spoon sauce over steaks; serve immediately. Serve with French-fried potatoes if desired. Makes 6 servings.

Note: If you use a less expensive cut of beef than strip sirloin, marinate steak overnight before cooking. Cook steak Diane quickly to retain tenderness. Always serve it on a heavy, preheated platter to keep the juices hot and to heighten the full flavor.

Exotic Steak

2	tablespoons oil	6 to 12 thin slices filet mignon
2	tablespoons butter	Salt
6	thick tomato slices	Pepper
4	cloves garlic, minced	
6	eggplant slices, sliced lengthwise	

Heat fat in skillet and sauté tomatoes and garlic over medium heat for 8 to 10 minutes, turning tomatoes from time to time. Remove tomatoes to heated platter and sauté eggplant in same skillet until tender and lightly browned on both sides. Place tomatoes back in pan. Season with salt and pepper. Keep very warm.

Heat another skillet. Sprinkle both sides of beef slices with salt and pepper and sauté them 1 minute on each side. Serve meat on heated platter surrounded with eggplant and tomato. Makes 6 servings.

Braised Steak Roll

Steaks Bercy

4	ounces softened butter	4	filet mignon steaks
1	tablespoon parsley, finely chopped	2	tablespoons vegetable oil
1	tablespoon chives, finely chopped	½	teaspoon salt
		⅛	teaspoon pepper
1	teaspoon dried chervil	4	lemon slices
1	teaspoon dried tarragon		Watercress
1	tablespoon shallots or onion, grated		French-fried potatoes (cut very thin, dried on towels, deep-fried)

Dash of pepper

Make herb butter first by blending softened butter, parsley, chives, chervil, tarragon, shallots, and pepper. Spoon onto sheet of waxed paper; shape into roll about 1-1/2 inches in diameter. Chill in freezer while steak is prepared. Cut into 4 thick slices just before serving.

Brush steaks with oil. Depending on thickness, broil about 5 minutes on each side or to desired doneness. Season with salt and pepper. Makes 4 servings.

Filets Mignons Rossini

2½ pounds filet beef (cut into 1- to 1½-inch-thick slices)	2 cups beef stock (or water and beef cube)
1 tablespoon butter or margarine	¼ cup red wine (optional)
2 tablespoons onions, chopped	Salt and pepper
	1 teaspoon chopped parsley and thyme
1 slice bacon, diced	1 cup butter
½ tablespoon flour	8 slices white bread
1 teaspoon tomato puree	1 cup cooking oil
8 large mushrooms, stems chopped	1 can pâté de foie gras
	Watercress

Preheat oven to 350°F.

First make sauce: Melt butter. Add onions and bacon. Slowly cook to golden color; stir well. Add flour; cook until just turning light brown. Add tomato puree, chopped mushrooms, stock, wine, salt, and pepper. Bring to boil; simmer 15 minutes. Add parsley and thyme; cook a few minutes. Strain through fine sieve into serving dish; keep warm.

Put mushroom tops into buttered dish; put small pat of butter, salt, and pepper on each. Cook in oven 10 minutes.

Cut bread into slices same size as filets. Heat oil; add 1 tablespoon butter. When foaming, fry bread until golden brown on both sides. Drain; keep warm.

Melt 1/2 cup butter in large frying pan. When foaming, cook filets 4 to 6 minutes each side, according to taste. (Or brush with melted butter and broil 5 to 8 minutes each side.)

Place filets on fried bread. Top each with slice of pâté and a mushroom. Spoon a little sauce over each steak; serve the rest separately. Garnish with watercress. Makes 8 servings.

Braised Steak Roll

1 pound round steak	1 level teaspoon mixed dried herbs
1 onion, chopped	
1 small can tomatoes	Salt and pepper
1 clove garlic, crushed	

Wipe meat with a clean damp cloth and place it between 2 pieces of wax paper. Beat it with a rolling pin until 1/4- to 1/2-inch thick.

Put all remaining ingredients into a saucepan, bring to a boil and boil rapidly, stirring occasionally, until thick. Spread tomato mixture over steak and roll up like a jelly roll. Wrap roll in foil and cook in a 325°F oven for 1-1/2 hours. Remove foil and cook for 30 minutes more. Serve cut into slices. Makes 3 to 4 servings.

Poor Man's Beef Stroganoff

Beef Flank Steak with Mushroom Stuffing

½ **teaspoon salt**	1 **tablespoon tomato paste**
¼ **teaspoon white pepper**	¼ **cup dried bread crumbs**
2 **pounds flank steak**	¼ **teaspoon salt**
1 **teaspoon Dijon-style mustard**	¼ **teaspoon pepper**
	1 **teaspoon paprika**

Mushroom Stuffing	*Gravy*
2 **tablespoons vegetable oil**	3 **strips bacon, cubed**
1 **small onion, chopped**	2 **small onions, finely chopped**
1 **(4-ounce) can mushroom pieces, drained and chopped**	1 **cup hot beef broth**
¼ **cup parsley, chopped**	1 **teaspoon Dijon-style mustard**
2 **tablespoons chives, chopped**	2 **tablespoons tomato catsup**

Lightly salt and pepper steak on both sides. Spread 1 side with mustard.

Prepare stuffing. Heat oil in frying pan. Add onion; cook 3 minutes, until lightly browned. Add mushrooms; cook 5 minutes. Stir in parsley, chives, tomato paste, and bread crumbs. Season with salt, pepper, and paprika. Spread stuffing on mustard side of steak. Roll up jelly-roll fashion; tie with thread or string.

Prepare gravy. Cook bacon in Dutch oven or heavy casserole until partially done. Add meat roll; brown on all sides, approximately 10 minutes. Add onions; sauté 5 minutes. Pour in beef broth; cover Dutch oven. Simmer 1 hour. Remove meat to preheated platter.

Season pan juices with mustard. Salt and pepper to taste; stir in catsup. Serve gravy separately. Makes 6 servings.

Steak and Mushroom Kabobs

1 **pound tenderloin steak**	2 **tablespoons catsup**
12 **small mushroom caps**	1 **teaspoon sugar**
½ **cup red wine**	½ **teaspoon salt**
½ **cup corn oil**	1 **tablespoon vinegar**
1 **teaspoon Worcestershire sauce**	**Pinch of dried marjoram**
1 **clove garlic, crushed**	**Pinch of dried rosemary**

Cut steak into small cubes. Mix all other ingredients together in bowl. Add steak; marinate at least 2 hours.

Alternate steak and mushrooms on skewers. Cook until meat is tender, about 15 minutes. Baste frequently with marinade. Makes about 8 skewers.

Beef Stew with Pastry Crust

Swiss Steak

2	pounds eye of round	1	large can tomatoes
½	cup flour	1	can tomato sauce
2	teaspoons salt	2 to 3 cups water
2	teaspoons paprika	½	teaspoon pepper
2	onions, sliced	½	cup shortening

Cut meat in slices about 3/8-inch thick. Dip into flour seasoned with salt and paprika.

Sauté onions until yellow. Remove onions with slotted spoon; leave fat in pan. Brown meat slices; remove from pan.

Put remaining seasoned flour into pan; stir. When flour and fat are mixed thoroughly, add boiling water. Stir until gravy is made. Add tomatoes and tomato sauce; if too thick, add more water. Bring to boil. Strain; pour over meat and onions that have been put into casserole.

Bake, tightly covered, in 325°F oven until meat is tender, approximately 2 hours. Serve over fluffy rice. Makes 8 servings.

Teriyaki Steak

4 boneless steaks, about ½
   pound each

Marinade
1 clove garlic, finely minced
1 sugared or candied ginger,
   finely minced
1 tablespoon brown sugar
Salt
Pepper, freshly ground
Pinch of monosodium
   glutamate (MSG)

½ cup red wine or sherry
6 tablespoons soy sauce
½ cup white wine
Juice of half a lemon

Stuffed-Tomato Garnish
4 medium-sized tomatoes
Salt
White pepper
4 tablespoons bean sprouts,
   canned or fresh
1 tablespoon tomato catsup

Combine marinade ingredients in shallow dish large enough to hold steaks. Stir until well blended. Add steaks; coat well. Marinate 12 hours; turn steaks frequently. Drain steaks; arrange on broiler pan. Place under preheated broiler; broil 4 minutes on each side.

Meanwhile, remove stems from tomatoes; cut off approximately 1/2-inch slices from bottoms. Scoop out seeds; discard. Sprinkle insides with salt and pepper.

Place bean sprouts and catsup into small skillet; heat 5 minutes. Spoon into tomatoes.

Arrange steaks on preheated serving platter. Garnish with stuffed tomatoes. Serve with rice. Makes 4 servings.

Note: If using fresh bean sprouts, boil 2 minutes, then rinse with cold water before using.

Beef Stroganoff

1 to 1½ pounds beef
   tenderloin
1 or 2 onions, thinly sliced
8 to 10 medium-sized
   mushrooms, thinly sliced

4 to 5 tablespoons butter
Salt and pepper
1 cup sour cream
Grated nutmeg

Cut beef into strips about 2-1/2 inches long and 1/2 inch thick.

Melt 2 tablespoons butter in frying pan; cook onions slowly until golden brown. Remove from pan; keep warm. Add a little more butter. Cook mushrooms about 5 minutes; add to onions.

Melt remaining butter. When foaming, put in about half the strips of steak. Fry quickly about 5 minutes, until brown on all sides. Remove; repeat with remaining steak.

Replace all meat and vegetables in pan. Shake over heat, adding salt, pepper, and nutmeg. Add sour cream; heat until it nearly boils. Serve immediately with plain boiled rice. Makes 4 servings.

Hamburger Stew with Green Peppers

Poor Man's Beef Stroganoff

1	pound top round steak	
6	tablespoons margarine	
½	cup beef stock or water and beef stock cube	
2	onions, thinly sliced	
½	cup mushrooms, sliced	
1	level tablespoon tomato puree	

Salt and pepper
¼ level teaspoon ground nutmeg
2 level teaspoons cornstarch
1 cup sour cream

Cut beef into thin strips about 2 inches long and 1/4 inch wide. Heat 4 tablespoons of margarine in large saucepan and fry steak until browned. Add stock and bring to a boil. Cover pan tightly. Simmer gently for 30 minutes.

Meanwhile, fry onions and mushrooms in remaining margarine until softened. Add them to beef with tomato puree, salt and pepper, and nutmeg. Cover pan again and continue cooking for 30 minutes or until beef is tender.

Mix cornstarch with a little water in a small bowl, then stir it into saucepan. Boil for 2 to 3 minutes. Remove from the heat and stir in sour cream. Serve over rice or noodles. Makes 4 servings.

Tenderloin Beef Wellington

4 to 5 tablespoons oil or shortening	1 onion, finely chopped
1 fillet tenderloin beef, 2 to 2½ pounds	1 cup mushrooms, finely chopped
1 clove garlic	2 tablespoons brandy
Pepper	1 tablespoon mixed herbs
3 tablespoons butter	1 package puff pastry
	1 egg

Heat oil or shortening. Rub over fillet with cut piece of garlic. Season with pepper. Roast in preheated 400°F oven about 20 to 25 minutes. Allow to cool. (Reset oven to 450°F for pastry.)

Melt butter. Cook onion and mushrooms 5 minutes, until onion is soft. Add brandy, seasoning, and herbs; let cool.

Roll pastry thinly on floured board to size that will completely cover tenderloin. Lay cooled meat in center; spoon mushroom-and-onion mixture over top. Brush pastry edges with water. Fold over top; pinch together to make pattern. Fold pastry carefully over ends to seal. Decorate with leaves made from leftover pastry. Brush whole surface with beaten egg, to glaze. Bake 20 to 30 minutes, until pastry is browned. Cut in slices to serve. Makes 4 servings.

Beef Stew with Pastry Crust

2½ pounds stew meat	2 cloves garlic, crushed
Butter for frying	2 teaspoons marjoram
1½ tablespoons flour	3 to 4 tablespoons red wine
1 teaspoon salt	2 to 3 teaspoons arrowroot, mixed with a little water
¼ teaspoon black pepper	Pimiento-filled olives, cut in half
1 large onion, chopped	
1 large eggplant, sliced and peeled	Snipped parsley
¼ pound fresh mushrooms	3 to 4 frozen pastry crust patties, just thawed
1 can crushed tomatoes	1 egg, beaten
1¼ cups beef broth	

Cut meat into 1-1/4-inch cubes, dredge them in flour, and brown them in butter in a frying pan. Season with salt and pepper. Place meat in a stew pot. Brown onion, eggplant, and mushrooms, each separately, in the frying pan, and place them in the stew pot. Add crushed tomatoes and broth. Bring to a boil and season with garlic and marjoram.

Simmer stew for about an hour, or until meat feels very tender. Season with red wine toward end of the simmering time. Thicken with arrowroot, which has been mixed with a little water, so that stew has a fine consistency.

Sunday Stew

Pour stew into ovenproof dish. Garnish with sliced olives and snipped parsley.

Place pastry crust patties together and roll them out into a 1/4-inch thick crust. Brush edges of pan with a beaten egg. Place crust over stew. Press well around edges of pan, make a hole in crust for steam to escape, and place in 400°F oven for about 20 to 25 minutes. Makes 6 servings.

Hamburger Stew with Green Peppers

1⅓ pounds ground chuck or ground round	2 to 3 tablespoons tomato paste
About 2½ tablespoons butter or margarine	4 to 5 green peppers
3 onions, peeled and chopped	1½ to 2 tablespoons snipped fresh thyme (or 1½ teaspoons dried thyme)
2 (14-ounce) cans crushed tomatoes	Dash cayenne pepper (optional)
2½ teaspoons salt	1 small beef bouillon cube (optional)
½ teaspoon ground black pepper	

Brown meat in a little butter or margarine in large frying pan or stew pot. Stir so that meat crumbles into little pieces. Peel and chop onions, and brown them with meat toward the end of browning process.

Place meat and onion in a stew pot if they have been browned in a frying pan. Add tomatoes, salt, pepper, and tomato paste. Cover and simmer over fairly low heat for 10 minutes.

In the meantime, remove seeds and membranes from peppers. Cut into thin strips, then divide strips into pieces. Add peppers and thyme to stew. Simmer stew for another 5 to 8 minutes so that peppers become somewhat soft.

Adjust seasoning if necessary; melt bouillon cube in stew, if desired, or if stew has a weak flavor. When served with noodles, stew might need to be thinned with a small amount of water. Makes 8 servings.

Sunday Stew

2 large onions	2 teaspoons paprika or chili powder
1 small piece celeriac (celery root)	1 bouillon cube
¾ pound ground meat	3 tablespoons tomato paste
About 1 teaspoon salt	About ¾ cup water
¼ teaspoon white or black pepper	Pasta (shells or penne)

Peel and chop onions and cut celeriac into small cubes. Brown meat in a pot while stirring, so that it evenly crumbles. Sauté onion and celeriac with the meat when the meat is almost all brown. Season and add bouillon cube, tomato paste, and water. Stir well and simmer for several minutes.

Prepare pasta according to the directions on the package (make enough for 4 servings). Add cooked pasta to stew. Makes 4 servings.

Stew with Vegetables and Meatballs

3	onions, peeled and sliced
6	potatoes, peeled and quartered
⅓	cup celeriac, cut in small cubes
2 to 3 carrots, thinly sliced
1	(14-ounce) can crushed tomatoes
⅓	cup vegetable broth
2	tablespoons tomato paste
1	teaspoon salt
½	teaspoon lemon pepper
¼	teaspoon cayenne pepper
1	green pepper, seeded and cut in strips
1	red pepper, seeded and chopped
1	leek, finely chopped

Meatballs

⅔ pound ground veal or hamburger meat
1 tablespoon bread crumbs
⅓ cup milk
½ teaspoon salt
⅛ teaspoon pepper
1 egg

Yogurt Salad

2 cups natural yogurt
¼ fresh cucumber
1 clove garlic, crushed
¼ teaspoon salt
⅛ teaspoon pepper

Place onion, potatoes, celeriac, and carrots in a pot. Add crushed tomatoes, broth, tomato paste, and spices, and simmer until vegetables begin to feel soft. Add peppers and leek.

Mix meatball ingredients together and shape them into small balls. Place them in vegetable stew and let them simmer with vegetables during the final 5 minutes.

Serve with yogurt salad. To make salad, drain yogurt for about 2 hours in a paper coffee filter. Grate cucumber coarsely and press as much liquid out of it as possible. Mix it with yogurt right before serving. Season with garlic, salt, and pepper. Makes 4 servings.

Chili Con Carne

2	tablespoons vegetable oil
½	cup onion, thinly sliced
½	cup green pepper, diced
1	clove garlic, crushed
¾	pound ground beef
¾	cup boiling water
1	can (about 20 ounces) peeled tomatoes

1 to 2 tablespoons chili powder (according to taste)
⅛ teaspoon paprika
Salt
2 cups canned kidney beans

Heat oil in kettle. Cook onion, pepper, and garlic about 10 minutes. Add meat. Increase heat; stir until meat has browned. Add water, tomatoes, chili powder, paprika, and a little salt. Cover; cook over low heat about 45

Corn Rolls

minutes. Add beans; cook 30 minutes. Adjust seasoning to taste before serving.

Eat with dry salted crackers or with rice. Makes 4 to 5 servings.

Filled Green Peppers

6 **green peppers**	**Pepper**
1 **pound ground beef**	1 **can crushed tomatoes**
Margarine or oil for frying	2 to 3 **teaspoons mixed herbs**
1 **whole garlic, peeled and**	**(oregano, basil, and**
chopped	**chervil)**
Salt	

Boil green peppers in salted, boiling water for 10 minutes. Cut a lid off each pepper and let peppers drain. Remove seeds.

Brown ground beef and garlic cloves in margarine for about 10 minutes. Season with salt and pepper, and pour mixture into a pot with crushed tomatoes. Simmer for 5 minutes. Season by adding oregano, basil, and chervil, according to your taste. Serve with boiled potatoes or rice. Makes 6 servings.

Corn Rolls

¾ **pound ground beef**	**6 to 8 ears fresh corn**
1 **large yellow onion, chopped**	1 **green pepper, chopped**
1 **(14-ounce) can crushed tomatoes**	**Herb salt**
	Black pepper
3 to 4 **tablespoons tomato paste**	2 **cups beef broth**

Place ground beef and onion in ungreased pan; brown. Add crushed tomatoes and tomato paste and let simmer for 25 minutes, stirring occasionally.

Shuck corn, but save husks. Scrape corn from cob and add it to ground beef mixture. Cut pepper into small bits and add. Season and let simmer a few minutes.

Rinse corn husks. You'll need several for each roll. Place a spoonful of ground beef mixture in center of a husk. Roll into tight package and fasten with toothpick. Place corn rolls together in shallow pan. Pour boiling bouillon over rolls. Cover and simmer for 15 minutes. Turn and baste after 7 minutes. Makes 4 servings.

Croquettes

1 **pound potatoes, boiled and mashed**	½ **teaspoon salt**
	⅛ **teaspoon white pepper**
1 **small onion, finely chopped**	**Tomato puree (optional)**
	2 to 3 **tablespoons flour**
2 to 3 **cups cooked ground beef**	2 **eggs, beaten**
	Dry white crumbs
1 **tablespoon chutney**	**Fat for deep frying**
1 **tablespoon chopped herbs**	**A bunch of parsley**

Mix potatoes and onion with meat, chutney, herbs, and seasoning. Add a little tomato puree if mixture is too dry. Put mixture on floured board. Make into long roll; cut into sections about 1 inch thick and 3 inches long. Roll in seasoned flour. Brush all over with eggs; roll in bread crumbs.

Deep-fry in smoking-hot fat until well browned; drain. Serve with parsley fried in deep fat a few seconds and pass a well-flavored sauce. Makes 4 servings.

Filled Green Pepper.

Gorgonzola-Filled Hamburgers

Ground beef	1 tablespoon Gorgonzola
Salt	cheese for each
Pepper	hamburger patty
Minced onion	Oil
Soda water	

Blend ground beef with salt, pepper, onion, and a little soda water. Fold so that all becomes well mixed.

Shape meat into hamburger patties. Make a hole in the middle of each patty and fill it with Gorgonzola cheese. Press meat around cheese so that it thoroughly covers cheese, and brush with oil.

Broil hamburgers for about 10 minutes on each side and serve with a mixed salad.

Ground Beef Gratin with Mushrooms

1 eggplant, pared	Black pepper
1 teaspoon salt	2 teaspoons paprika
About 2 cups fresh	1 to 1¼ cups boiled rice
mushrooms, rinsed and	1 onion, finely chopped
chopped	1 green pepper, cubed
1 tablespoon margarine	¾ cup broth
1 pound ground beef	About 1 cup cheese, coarsely
1 teaspoon salt	grated

Cut eggplant into slices and place on bottom of a greased, ovenproof dish. Season with salt. Sauté mushrooms in margarine until liquid has soaked back into the vegetables. Place mushrooms over eggplant.

Mix ground beef with salt, pepper, and paprika. Add boiled rice, which has been allowed to become cold, and onion. Add green pepper and broth. The beef should be rather loose in consistency.

Spread meat out in the dish. Sprinkle with grated cheese. Place dish in preheated 350°F oven for about 30 minutes, or until meat is cooked through. Makes 4 servings.

Gorgonzola-Filled Hamburgers

Barbecued Meatballs

Meatballs
1   **pound ground beef**
¾   **cup bread crumbs**
½   **cup milk**
½   **cup onions, chopped**
1   **teaspoon salt**
½   **teaspoon pepper**
½   **teaspoon oregano**
1   **egg**

Barbecue Sauce
1   **(10½-ounce) can tomato puree**
¼   **cup molasses**
¼   **cup brown sugar**
¼   **cup vinegar**
1   **teaspoon sweet basil**

Combine meatball ingredients; form into 1-inch meatballs. Brown in skillet; drain.

Combine the sauce ingredients. Simmer, covered, in skillet used for meatballs, about 15 minutes to allow flavors to blend. Delicious over rice or noodles. Makes 3 to 4 servings.

Ground Beef Gratin with Mushrooms

Hawaiian Sweet-and-Sour Meatballs

1½ **pounds ground beef**	1¼ **cups pineapple juice**
2 **eggs**	1 **tablespoon soy sauce**
4 **tablespoons cornstarch**	3 **tablespoons vinegar**
1 **onion, minced**	⅓ **cup water**
¼ **teaspoon pepper**	½ **cup brown sugar**
¼ **teaspoon nutmeg**	2 **cups fresh pineapple and**
1 **teaspoon salt**	**papaya chunks**
¼ **teaspoon garlic powder or**	2 **green peppers, cut into**
minced garlic	**bite-sized pieces**
2 **tablespoons salad oil**	

Blend beef, eggs, 1 teaspoon cornstarch, onion, pepper, nutmeg, salt, and garlic together. Form into 1-inch balls. Heat oil in skillet; brown meatballs on all sides.

In large saucepan, add remaining cornstarch, soy sauce, vinegar, water, and brown sugar to pineapple juice. Cook until thickened, stirring constantly. Add meatballs, fruit, and peppers. Cook 5 minutes or until fruit is well heated. Makes 4 to 6 servings.

Meatballs Königsberg-Style

Meatballs
1 hard roll
¾ cup water
1 pound lean ground beef
1 strip bacon, diced
4 anchovy fillets, diced
1 small onion, chopped
1 egg
½ teaspoon salt
¼ teaspoon white pepper

Broth
6 cups water
½ teaspoon salt
1 bay leaf

1 small onion, peeled and halved
6 peppercorns

Gravy
1½ tablespoons butter or margarine
1½ tablespoons flour
1 tablespoon capers, drained
Juice of ½ lemon
½ teaspoon prepared mustard
1 egg yolk
¼ teaspoon salt
¼ teaspoon white pepper

Soak roll in water about 10 minutes. Squeeze dry; place in mixing bowl with ground beef. Add bacon, anchovy fillets, onion, egg, salt, and pepper; mix thoroughly.

Prepare broth by boiling water seasoned with salt, bay leaf, onion, and peppercorns.

Shape meat mixture into balls about 2 inches in diameter. Add to boiling broth; simmer over low heat 20 minutes. Remove meatballs with slotted spoon. Set aside; keep warm. Strain broth through sieve. Reserve broth; keep warm.

To prepare gravy, heat butter in frying pan; stir in flour. Cook 3 minutes, stirring constantly. Slowly blend in 2 cups reserved broth. Add capers, lemon juice, and mustard; simmer 5 minutes.

Remove a small amount of sauce to blend with egg yolk. Stir egg yolk back into sauce. Season with salt and pepper.

Place reserved meatballs into gravy; reheat if necessary. Serve on a preheated platter. Makes 4 servings.

German Meat Loaf

1 **pound ground beef**	¼ **teaspoon pepper**
1 **egg**	1 **small head cauliflower**
¼ **cup milk**	1 **cup sharp Cheddar cheese,**
⅓ **cup dry bread crumbs**	**grated**
½ **cup onion, chopped**	1 **cup evaporated milk**
½ **teaspoon salt**	3 **tomatoes, halved**
1 **teaspoon Worcestershire**	
sauce	

Mix beef, egg, milk, crumbs, onion, and seasonings to make meat loaf. Mold into ring in 2-quart-round baking dish.

Parboil cauliflower 5 minutes. Place in center of meat loaf. Mix cheese and milk, pour over cauliflower.

Bake at 350°F 45 minutes to 1 hour. Last 5 minutes of baking, place tomatoes on top of meat loaf. Makes 4 servings.

Potato Coated Meat Loaf

1 **pound ground beef**	1 **onion, finely chopped or**
½ **cup fresh bread crumbs**	**grated**
½ **cup cold milk**	1 **pound potatoes**
1 **egg, beaten**	2 **tablespoons butter or**
Salt and pepper	**margarine**
¼ **level teaspoon cayenne**	**Hot milk to mix**
pepper	2 **level tablespoons parsley,**
¼ **level teaspoon dry mustard**	**chopped**

Put ground beef in a mixing bowl with bread crumbs, cold milk, egg, 1 level teaspoon salt, cayenne pepper, mustard, and onion. Mix all together very thoroughly. Put in a greased 1-pound loaf pan and bake in a 350°F oven for 45 minutes.

Meanwhile, peel potatoes and cook in boiling salted water until tender (about 15 to 20 minutes). Mash well with butter and enough hot milk to make creamy mashed potatoes. Beat in salt, pepper, and 1 tablespoon parsley.

Turn cooked meat loaf out of tin and put it on a baking tray. Coat loaf in mashed potatoes and return it to oven for about 15 minutes or until beginning to brown. Serve garnished with chopped parsley. Makes 4 servings.

Beef Roll

1 **pound ground beef**	½ **cup milk or beef stock**
Salt and pepper	1 **small package frozen**
½ **level teaspoon mixed dried**	**mixed vegetables**
herbs	4 **tablespoons catsup**
¼ **cup soft bread crumbs**	**Parsley for garnish**
1 **large onion, grated**	

Put ground beef into a mixing bowl with salt and pepper, herbs, bread crumbs, onions, and milk or stock. Mix very thoroughly. Put meat mixture onto a piece of foil and pat out gently to a 9-inch square. Spread mixed vegetables on the meat and roll up like a jelly roll. Fold foil around the roll securely. Then seal ends together.

Put on a baking tray and cook in a 350°F oven for 30 minutes. Unwrap foil and spread on the catsup. Continue cooking for a further 30 minutes. Serve garnished with parsley. Makes 4 servings.

Potato Coated Meat Loaf

Stuffed Bacon with Ground Meat

1 **pound ground chuck**	2 **tablespoons red wine**
1 **tablespoon onion,** **chopped**	1 **tablespoon black currant** **juice or jelly**
1 **tablespoon parsley,** **chopped**	1 **teaspoon thyme**
3 **tablespoons heavy cream**	1 **teaspoon arrowroot mixed** **with a little water**
½ **teaspoon salt**	1 **teaspoon lemon juice**
Pepper	**(optional)**
¼ **pound sliced bacon**	**Orange peel**
Juice from 1 orange	**Finely chopped parsley**
1 to 1¼ **cups beef broth**	

Mix meat, onion, parsley, and cream together. Season with salt and pepper and form into rolls. Wrap the rolls up in thin bacon slices.

Fry stuffed bacon slowly in a frying pan until evenly brown. Add orange juice, broth, red wine, and currant juice or jelly. Season with thyme, salt, pepper, and lemon juice. Thicken with arrowroot mixed with a little water. Simmer for 4 to 5 minutes. Heat up thin strips of orange peel in sauce. Sprinkle with parsley when it is time to serve the meal. Makes 4 servings.

Stuffed Chilies

2 **medium-sized onions,** **chopped**	½ **teaspoon pepper**
1 **clove garlic, crushed**	4 **tablespoons almonds,** **sliced**
2 **tablespoons oil**	4 **tablespoons raisins**
½ **pound ground beef**	8 **whole canned chilies**
½ **pound ground pork**	½ **cup flour**
1 **cup fresh tomatoes,** **chopped**	4 **eggs**
1 **teaspoon salt**	**Oil for frying**

Sauté onions and garlic in 2 tablespoons oil until onion is transparent. Add ground meats; stir until meat is crumbly. Add chopped tomatoes, seasonings, almonds, and raisins; simmer.

Remove chili seeds; leave skins whole. Stuff with meat filling; roll well in flour. Dip in following egg batter: Beat egg whites until stiff; beat egg yolks. Combine egg yolks with egg whites.

Fry chilies in deep fat at 375°F until golden brown. Remove; drain on paper towels. Makes 8 servings.

Beef Roll

Mock Stroganoff

1	pound ground beef	2	tablespoons sherry
¼	cup onion, chopped	½	cup sour cream
1	clove garlic, crushed		Salt
1	can condensed cream of		Cooked noodles or rice
	mushroom soup		Chopped parsley
⅓	cup milk		

Lightly brown meat in skillet with onion and garlic, stirring. Add soup and milk; heat well, stirring. Reduce heat; stir in sherry, then sour cream. Season to taste.

Serve over noodles; garnish with parsley. Makes 4 to 6 servings.

Tamale Pie

½ **pound ground beef**	1 **teaspoon salt**
½ **pound bulk pork sausage**	¼ **teaspoon pepper**
1 **large onion, sliced**	
⅛ **teaspoon garlic, minced**	***Cornmeal Pastry***
1 **(16-ounce) can tomatoes**	1 **cup cornmeal**
with juice	2 **medium eggs**
1 **(12-ounce) can whole-**	1 **cup milk**
kernel corn, drained	18 **green olives, chopped**
1 **tablespoon chili powder**	**Olive slices for garnish**

Cook meats with onion and garlic until browned. Stir in tomatoes with juice, corn, and seasonings. Simmer 10 minutes. Pour into greased oblong baking dish.

Prepare cornmeal crust by mixing cornmeal, eggs, milk, and chopped olives. Spread over hot mixture. Decorate top with few olive slices. Bake at 350°F 30 to 35 minutes. Serve tamale pie warm. Makes 4 to 6 servings.

Bacon and Kidney Stuffed Potatoes

4 **large potatoes**	**Salt and pepper**
4 **rashers streaky bacon**	2 **tablespoons margarine**
4 **lambs' kidneys**	**Watercress for garnish**

Scrub potatoes and bake in 400°F oven for 1 hour or until cooked (test with a pointed knife).

Place bacon on a board and remove rinds and any bones, then flatten each one with a round-bladed knife. Cut kidneys in half lengthways and remove skin. Cut away white core with a sharp knife or pair of scissors. Wrap 2 kidney halves in each rasher of bacon.

Cut off top of the potatoes and scoop out enough hot potato to make room for the kidney and bacon roll. Sprinkle a little salt and pepper into each one with a pat of margarine. Put in kidneys and pack them in with the scooped-out potato; replace the tops.

Return potatoes to oven for a further 20 to 25 minutes, or until kidneys are cooked. After 15 minutes in the oven, remove potato lids to allow bacon to crisp. Place each potato in a table napkin, garnish with watercress, and serve hot. Makes 4 servings.

Stuffed Bacon with Ground Meat

Risotto alla Bolognese

2 to 3 tablespoons butter	1 dessert spoon tomato puree
1 onion, finely chopped	2½ to 3 cups stock
1 clove garlic, crushed	Salt and pepper
½ to ¾ pound calf liver, cut into chunks	1 tablespoon mixed herbs
1 cup mushrooms, quartered	1 cup Parmesan cheese, grated
1 cup long-grain rice	

Melt butter; cook onion and garlic a few minutes with lid on pan. Add liver; cook quickly until it changes color. Remove from heat.

Add mushrooms, rice, tomato puree, 2-1/2 cups stock, salt, and pepper. Bring to a boil; stir all the time. Reduce heat; simmer gently 25 to 30 minutes. Stir occasionally;, add extra stock if rice becomes dry. When cooked, rice should have absorbed all moisture. Sprinkle top with chopped herbs. Serve with grated cheese. Makes 4 servings.

Braised Liver and Onions

1½ **pounds beef liver, sliced**	¼ **teaspoon pepper**
½ **cup flour**	1 **large onion, sliced**
2 **tablespoons fat or oil**	¼ **cup water**
1½ **teaspoons salt**	

Remove skin and large veins from liver; coat with flour.

Heat fat in large frying pan over moderate heat; brown liver on one side. Turn liver; sprinkle with seasonings. Cover with onion. Add water; cover pan tightly. Cook over low heat 20 to 30 minutes or until liver is tender. Makes 6 servings.

Red-Stewed Beef Tongue

1 **small fresh beef tongue (2 pounds)**	2 **tablespoons cooking wine**
Boiling water to cover meat	2 **tablespoons dark soy sauce per pound of meat**
½ **clove garlic**	1 **teaspoon sugar per pound of meat**
1 **tablespoon oil**	

Immerse tongue completely in boiling water. Turn off heat; let soak 1 minute. Remove tongue from water. Use blunt knife to peel off skin and trim base.

Brown garlic in oil in wok or skillet. Brown tongue on both sides. Lower heat; add cooking wine. For each pound of tongue, add 2 tablespoons dark soy sauce. Cook over low heat 1-1/2 to 2 hours. Turn tongue at 20-minute intervals. Add water to maintain quantity of cooking liquid at 6 to 8 tablespoons. During last 20 minutes, add 1 teaspoon of sugar per pound. Makes 4 servings.

Braised Oxtails

3 **tablespoons butter or fat**	2 **tablespoons flour**
1 **onion, chopped**	2 **oxtails**
2 **carrots, sliced**	1 **teaspoon salt**
1 **small turnip, diced**	⅛ **teaspoon pepper**
1 **stalk celery, chopped**	2 **cloves**

Melt butter in saucepan. Add onion, carrots, turnip, and celery. When very lightly browned, stir in flour; blend well.

Cut oxtails into 2- to 3-inch pieces; add to pan. Add salt, pepper, cloves, and 2 cups water. Bring to boil, stirring constantly. Reduce heat; let simmer 2 to 3 hours.

Serve oxtails hot with liquid for gravy. Makes 6 to 8 servings.

Oxtail Casserole

1	cup dried butterbeans	2	strips streaky bacon, chopped
1	large oxtail		
½	cup flour	2	carrots, sliced
Salt and pepper		1	level teaspoon mixed dried herbs
2	tablespoons oil or beef drippings		
		2	cups water
2	onions, chopped	1	small package frozen peas

Soak butterbeans overnight in cold water to cover. Ask your butcher to chop oxtail in pieces. Season flour with salt and pepper and coat oxtail pieces.

Heat oil or drippings in saucepan and fry onion, bacon, and carrot, stirring until softened. Drain and put into ovenproof casserole.

Fry oxtail until browned all over. Drain and put into the casserole. Sprinkle with herbs and add water and butterbeans. Cover casserole and put into 325°F oven for 2-1/2 hours. Add peas and continue cooking for a further 30 minutes. This recipe improves by being kept overnight. Remove any fat before reheating. Makes 4 to 6 servings.

Bacon and Kidney Stuffed Potatoes

Lamb

Apricot-Mint Lamb

1	(6-pound) leg of lamb	1	cup boiling water
2	teaspoons salt		(approximately)
¼	teaspoon ground black pepper	½	cup apricot preserves
		½	teaspoon mint flavoring
1	large onion or 1 teaspoon onion powder	¼	teaspoon summer savory
		½	cup dry sherry
¼	teaspoon garlic powder	1	teaspoon arrowroot
1	bouillon cube, dissolved in 1 cup water		

Rub leg of lamb well with salt; brown on all sides in roasting pan over moderately high heat. Drain most of fat from pan. Blend pepper, onion, garlic, and bouillon into remaining pan drippings; stir together well.

Mix boiling water, preserves, mint flavoring, and summer savory. Stir into bouillon mixture; add sherry. Roast in 350°F oven 20 to 30 minutes per pound; baste as needed. Blend arrowroot into pan liquid 30 minutes before removing from pan. Cook and stir often until sauce thickens. Makes 8 to 10 servings.

California Stuffed Breast of Lamb

4 to 5 tablespoons butter	1 egg, beaten
1 cup onion, chopped	Salt and pepper
½ cup celery, chopped	3 pounds breast lamb
1½ cups fresh white bread	without bones
crumbs	Garlic powder
½ cup raisins	2 tablespoons seasoned flour
1 teaspoon sugar	2 to 3 tablespoons oil
3 oranges	1 cup stock
1 lemon	

Make stuffing. Melt butter; cook onion and celery slowly until soft without browning. Mix into bread crumbs; add raisins, sugar, and grated rind of 2 oranges and 1 lemon. Add juice of lemon and egg; season with salt and pepper. Add sections of 2 oranges; mix well. Let stand a few minutes before using.

Flatten lamb; dust over with garlic powder. Spread orange stuffing evenly over meat about 1/4 inch thick. (Any left over can be cooked separately in buttered dish.) Roll meat tightly; tie in 3 or 4 places with white string. Roll in seasoned flour.

Preheat oven to 350°F. Warm oil in baking pan in oven. Add lamb; baste well. Cook in preheated 350°F oven 1-1/2 hours; baste every 15 minutes. For last 10 minutes turn up oven to 400°F to brown outside of roll. When meat is tender and cooked through, remove; keep warm on serving dish.

Pour away excess fat; reserve juices. Add 1 teaspoon flour; mix well. Add stock and grated rind and juice of 1 orange; bring to boil. Season; serve. Makes 4 servings.

Stuffed Lamb Chops

6 double-rib lamb chops	¼ cup dry sherry wine
1 (3-ounce) can mushroom	1 egg, beaten
slices, drained	½ cup bread crumbs
2 tablespoons mushroom	¼ teaspoon white pepper
liquid	
1 teaspoon salt	

Using sharp knife, make slit from bone side between rib bones into center of meat on each chop.

Drain mushrooms; reserve 2 tablespoons liquid. Mix together reserved mushroom liquid, 1/2 teaspoon salt, sherry, egg, mushrooms, and bread crumbs. Stuff chops with mixture. Sprinkle with 1/2 teaspoon salt and pepper. Broil chops 4 to 5 inches from flame 12 minutes on each side. Serve immediately. Makes 6 servings.

Lamb Chops with Herbs on Grill

4 **large loin or 8 rib lamb chops**	**Grated rind and juice of 1 lemon**
1 **teaspoon thyme**	**Pinch of paprika**
1 **teaspoon oregano**	6 **tablespoons oil**
1 **teaspoon rosemary**	**Salt and pepper**
3 **small bay leaves, crushed**	**Butter**
6 **coriander seeds, crushed**	

Trim chops of excess fat.

Mix herbs, lemon rind, and paprika. Rub mixture well into both sides of chops. Arrange chops in large shallow dish; pour lemon juice and oil over them. Season lightly with salt and pepper; set aside in cool place about 3 hours, turning occasionally.

When ready to cook, drain chops well; put on grid over hot coals. Turn once or twice while cooking; allow about 16 to 20 minutes.

If any dried herbs are left over, a good pinch sprinkled over hot coals just before removal of chops will give delicious aroma and improve flavor.

Serve chops with pat of butter on each and plain tossed salad. Makes 4 servings.

Curry Lamb Ragout

1 **pound lean lamb meat**	1 **green pepper, cut into strips**
2 **tablespoons vegetable oil**	1 **(8-ounce) can sliced mushrooms, drained**
½ **teaspoon sage**	
Grated rind of half a lemon	2 **tomatoes, peeled and quartered**
1 **medium-sized onion, chopped**	1 **tart apple, peeled, cored and coarsely chopped**
2 **cups beef bouillon**	
1 **tablespoon curry powder**	½ **cup plain yogurt**
½ **teaspoon salt**	
⅛ **teaspoon white pepper**	

Cut meat into 1-inch cubes.

Heat oil in heavy saucepan or Dutch oven. Add meat, sage, and lemon rind; brown meat on all sides. Add onion; sauté lightly. Drain off excess oil; stir in bouillon. Cover saucepan; simmer 50 minutes.

Season with curry, salt, and pepper. Add green pepper; simmer, uncovered, 5 minutes. Stir in mushrooms, tomatoes, and apple; simmer 5 minutes. Cool mixture slightly; gradually add yogurt. Heat thoroughly without boiling; serve at once. Makes 4 servings.

Lamb Curry with Prunes

Lamb Curry with Prunes

⅔ **cup prunes**	1 **level tablespoon curry**
1½ **pounds boned shoulder of**	**powder or to taste**
lamb	1 **level teaspoon ground**
2 **tablespoons margarine**	**ginger**
2 **onions, chopped**	**Salt and pepper**
1 **clove garlic, crushed**	

Put prunes in bowl and cover with 3/4 pint boiling water. Soak for 2 hours. Cut meat into 1-inch cubes.

Heat margarine in heavy-based saucepan; add onion and garlic and fry gently until tender, stirring frequently. Stir in lamb and fry until browned all over. Stir in curry powder and ginger and fry gently for 3 minutes, stirring continuously. Stir in prunes, the soaking water, and salt and pepper to taste. Bring to a boil, cover pan, and simmer gently for 1-1/2 hours or until meat is tender, stirring occasionally.

Leave to cool, then place in refrigerator overnight. Next day, reheat thoroughly. Serve with boiled rice. Makes 4 to 6 servings

Oxtail Casserole

Lamb with Dill

About 2½ pounds lamb meat with the bone—shoulder, breast, rib
Water
2 teaspoons salt per quart of water
Dill stalks
6 white peppercorns
2 cloves garlic, unpeeled
1 small carrot, cut into small pieces
1 leek or onion, cut into small pieces

Sauce
1½ tablespoons butter or margarine
2½ tablespoons flour
1⅔ to 2 cups broth
3 tablespoons snipped dill
1 tablespoon pressed lemon juice
1 egg yolk
¼ cup cream

Place meat in a pot. Measure and pour over as much water as needed to cover meat. Add salt and bring to a boil. Skim well and add dill, pepper, garlic, carrot, and leek or onion. Let meat simmer over low heat until it feels tender, 1 to 1-1/2 hours.

To make sauce, melt butter in a pot, stir in flour, and dilute with the broth. Let sauce boil for several minutes. Season with dill and lemon juice.

Remove pot from heat and add yolk, which has first been beaten with the cream. The sauce should not be allowed to boil again as it can curdle.

Cut up meat and serve it with sauce, boiled potatoes, and vegetables. Makes 4 servings.

Mini Lamb Rolls

About 2½ pounds thin breast of lamb
Salt
Pepper
1 bunch parsley
1 bunch chives
1 teaspoon salt
¼ teaspoon ground black pepper

½ teaspoon thyme
1 large piece celeriac (celery root)
2 medium-sized onions, cut into large pieces
About 1 cup broth
1 tablespoon butter

Preheat oven to 400°F. Remove bones from lamb breast. Take away largest membranes and cut straight across where the bone sits, making 3 to 4 inch-wide strips. Cut these strips down the middle.

Salt and pepper meat. Chop chives and parsley; mix with thyme, and sprinkle this mixture evenly over meat.

Cut celeriac into 1/2-inch thick strips. Place 1 strip on each piece of meat. Roll meat strips up tightly into small mini-rolls and fasten them securely with a toothpick.

Brown rolls on all sides in butter, then place them in a greased ovenproof dish or pot. Add onions. Pour in hot broth, cover, and place in oven for about an hour. Add rest of celeriac stalks when about 15 minutes of the baking time remains. Serve with boiled potatoes, sprinkled with snipped parsley or chives. Makes 4 servings.

Grilled Piquant Leg of Lamb

1 (5-pound) leg of lamb
Vegetable oil
Salt
½ teaspoon freshly ground pepper
½ cup water
½ cup red wine
2 tablespoons wine vinegar

1 tablespoon Worcestershire sauce
¼ cup lemon juice
1 teaspoon dry mustard
Dash of hot sauce
¼ teaspoon paprika
1 clove garlic, pressed
1 medium onion, grated

Rub lamb with 1 tablespoon oil, 1 tablespoon salt, and pepper. Place on grill over low coals or in 325°F oven; cook about 3/4 to 1 hour. Turn occasionally; brush with oil.

Combine water, wine, vinegar, Worcestershire sauce, lemon juice, mustard, hot sauce, paprika, garlic, onion, 1 tablespoon oil, and 1/2 teaspoon salt in saucepan; bring to boil. Brush lamb with sauce; cook about 1 hour, to desired degree of doneness. Turn occasionally; brush with sauce. If using oven, turn on broiler after final brushing to glaze slightly. Makes about 10 servings.

Lamb Kebabs

1	small knuckle end shoulder of lamb	
2	lambs' kidneys	
2	onions	
1	small green pepper (optional)	
4	tomatoes	
8	mushrooms	

Marinade

2	tablespoons oil
2	tablespoons vinegar
¼	level teaspoon dried mixed herbs
¼	level teaspoon sugar
¼	level teaspoon dry mustard
1	clove garlic, crushed
	Salt and pepper

Cut meat from the bone into 8 (1-inch) cubes and put into a bowl. Remove skin and cores of kidneys and cut each into 4 pieces. Peel onions and cut each into eighths. Blanch pepper (if used) in boiling water for 3 minutes; cut into 8 pieces and remove seeds. Skin tomatoes and halve them. Remove stalks from mushrooms. Place all vegetables in the bowl with lamb and kidneys.

Make marinade by putting all ingredients into a screw-top jar and shaking well. Pour marinade over lamb and vegetables, leave to marinate for at least 4 hours, stirring occasionally.

Thread lamb and vegetables alternately onto 4 skewers. Baste with marinade and broil, basting and turning frequently for about 15 minutes or until cooked. Serve with mounds of rice. Makes 4 servings.

Barbecued Stuffed Leg of Lamb

1	onion, chopped
½	cup dried apricots, chopped and soaked
3	tablespoons raisins, chopped
3	tablespoons dates, chopped
2	tablespoons nuts, chopped
5	tablespoons cooked rice
2	tablespoons parsley, chopped
1	teaspoon marjoram, chopped

	Little lemon rind and juice
	Salt and pepper
1	leg of lamb, weighing 3 pounds after removal of bone
	Little strong stock
1	clove garlic, slivered
	Oil
	Barbecue spice or barbecue sauce

Mix onion with apricots, raisins, and dates. Add nuts, rice, parsley, marjoram, lemon rind and juice, salt, pepper and enough stock to moisten. Fill stuffing into lamb cavity left by removal of bones; sew up slits. Insert garlic into small shallow slits cut into surface of lamb with point of sharp knife.

Put lamb onto rod of spit; spoon oil over surface. Season well with salt, pepper, and barbecue spice or barbecue sauce. Cook about 1-1/2 hours, until meat is tender and browned; baste with oil and seasoning when necessary. Makes 4 to 6 servings.

Make sauce with liquids from lamb and some stock and seasoning.

Roast Leg of Lamb

1	**(6-pound) leg of lamb**	1	**bay leaf**
3	**teaspoons salt**	1	**teaspoon instant minced**
¼	**teaspoon pepper**		**onion**
2	**tablespoons flour**		

Wipe lamb with damp cloth; do not remove fell. Combine salt and pepper; rub all over meat. Insert meat thermometer into fleshy part away from bone. Place on rack in shallow roasting pan. Roast, uncovered, in a preheated 325°F oven 2-1/2 to 3 hours, until meat thermometer reads 175°F for medium lamb, 180°F for well-done. Remove to heated platter, keep warm.

Make gravy. Pour off drippings; reserve 2 tablespoons in roasting pan. Stir in flour until smooth; gradually stir in 2 cups cold water. Add bay leaf and onion; bring to boiling, stirring constantly. Reduce heat; simmer 5 minutes. Serve hot in gravy boat, along with lamb. Makes 6 to 8 servings.

Lamb with Dill

Crown Roast of Lamb with Onion and Apple Stuffing

2 **racks (6 or 7 bones each) best end of neck lamb cutlets**	1 **level teaspoon salt**
2 **tablespoons margarine**	¼ **level teaspoon pepper**
1 **onion, chopped**	1 **level teaspoon dried sage**
2 **dessert apples, peeled and diced**	⅓ **cup soft white bread crumbs**
	1 **egg**
	Water to mix

Make the 2 racks of cutlets into a 'crown' or ask your butcher to do this for you. (Order the 'crown' well in advance and the butcher will be more obliging.) If you are doing it at home, cut and scrape the meat away from the bones 1 inch from the top. Wrap the tops in foil to prevent them becoming too brown. Stitch the 2 racks of cutlets together with thin string to make a circle.

Melt margarine in a saucepan and fry onion and apple until softened. Stir in remaining ingredients, adding enough water to moisten the stuffing.

Put crown of lamb onto a baking tray and pile stuffing into the center. Weigh the meat and stuffing. Roast in a 375°F oven for 20 minutes per pound, plus 20 minutes over. Remove the foil and replace with cutlet frills if liked. Makes 6 to 12 servings.

Stuffed Crown Roast of Lamb

Crown of lamb, at least 2 ribs per person	1 **onion, chopped**
Oil for roasting	3 to 4 **tablespoons butter**
Salt and pepper	¼ **cup almonds skinned, sliced and slightly browned**
1 to 1½ **cups cooked rice**	
½ **cup cooked peas**	
½ **cup cooked corn**	½ **cup raisins**
¼ **cup cooked red and green sweet peppers, chopped**	2 to 3 **tablespoons sherry**
	Chopped mixed herbs

Have butcher prepare roast; allow 16 ribs to make a nice-sized roast. Cover tips of rib bones with foil to prevent burning; crumble some foil into center of roast to preserve shape while roasting.

Heat 2 to 3 tablespoons oil in roasting pan; put in roast. Baste with hot fat; put into preheated 450°F oven. After 10 minutes reduce heat to 350°F; cook 20 to 25 minutes per pound. Season with salt and pepper; baste every 15 minutes.

Meanwhile, prepare stuffing. Boil rice. When cooked and drained, mix in peas, corn, and peppers.

Cook onion gently in butter until golden brown. Add to rice, along with almonds and raisins which have been soaked in a little sherry. Add seasoning and herbs.

When crown roast is cooked, remove from oven; put on serving dish. Remove foil; fill center with rice stuffing. Decorate chop bones with paper or foil frills; serve roast with green vegetable and gravy made with roasting juices and red currant jelly. Carve down between bones; allow 2 per person. Makes 6 to 8 servings.

Mini Lamb Rolls

Peninsula Lamb Shanks

6	(1-pound) lamb shanks	1	clove garlic, finely minced
1½	teaspoons salt	4	cups celery, sliced
¼	teaspoon pepper	3	medium-sized tomatoes,
3	tablespoons oil		cut into wedges
3	tablespoons flour	1	tablespoon parsley,
1	(14-ounce) can chicken		chopped
	broth		
1	medium-sized onion,		
	sliced		

Sprinkle lamb with salt and pepper. Heat oil in Dutch oven. Add lamb; brown well on all sides. Remove lamb; set aside.

Stir flour into oil; brown lightly. Gradually blend in broth and 1-3/4 cups water; bring to boil. Return lamb to Dutch oven; add onion and garlic. Reduce heat; cover. Simmer 1-1/4 to 1-1/2 hours, until lamb is tender; remove lamb to warm serving platter.

Add celery to liquid in Dutch oven; cook 10 minutes. Add tomatoes and parsley; cook 5 minutes. Spoon over lamb. Makes 6 servings.

Lamb with Vegetables

1	large onion, chopped	Water
1	large carrot, sliced	Salt
2	large leeks, sliced	Pepper
Butter or oil		Mustard seeds
1	large meaty lamb roast	Bay leaf
1	can consommé plus 1	Sprigs of parsley
	bouillon cube	

Brown onion, carrot, and leeks in butter or oil in a thick-bottomed pot. Insert a cooking thermometer in the well-trimmed lamb roast. Place roast on the vegetables, cover with consommé, bouillon cube, and enough water to come more than halfway up the roast. Salt lightly, season with pepper, mustard seeds, bay leaf, and sprigs of parsley. Cover and cook slowly until thermometer shows 150 to 160°F. Remove roast, wrap it up in aluminum foil, and keep it warm.

Strain roast juice and simmer it so that it becomes a thick gravy. Then mix in more mustard seeds to make a strong sauce.

Serve roast with potato cakes and applesauce. Makes 10 servings.

Lamb Kebabs

Skewered Lamb

¼ cup onion, minced	16 small boiling onions, peeled
1 clove garlic, minced	
3 tablespoons olive oil	16 mushrooms, cleaned and stems removed
3 tablespoons lemon juice	
1 teaspoon salt	2 red peppers, cut into chunks
¼ teaspoon pepper	
½ teaspoon dried oregano, crumbled	
1½ pounds leg of lamb or lamb shoulder meat, cut into 2-inch cubes	

Combine minced onion, garlic, oil, lemon juice, salt, pepper, and oregano in glass bowl or casserole. Add lamb; stir well. Cover; marinate 3 to 4 hours (or longer in refrigerator), stirring occasionally.

Parboil 16 onions in salted water 10 minutes. Drain; cool.

Drain lamb; reserve marinade. Skewer vegetables and lamb alternately (lamb cube, onion, mushroom, and pepper chunk; repeat). Cook over charcoal or in broiler about 15 minutes; brush frequently with marinade. Serve with rice. Makes 4 servings.

Variation: Substitute cherry tomatoes and green peppers for red peppers. Skewer onions and meat alternately. Skewer vegetables separately; brush them with marinade. Tomatoes can be grilled only a short time or they will fall off skewer before meat is done. Start meat first; add skewered vegetables 5 minutes before meat is finished.

Lamb Stew

1½ to 2 pounds lamb meat with bone—back, shoulder, or cracked breast	Slightly less than 1 teaspoon thyme
	¼ cup parsley, chopped
8 small onions	¼ cup snipped chives
4 tomatoes, cut into pieces	1 to 1¼ cups broth
About 1 teaspoon salt	1 tablespoon flour
½ teaspoon black pepper	⅓ cup crème fraîche or sour cream
1 to 2 cloves garlic, crushed	

Cut meat into pieces and brown them in a small amount of butter in a frying pan. Pour into a stewing pot. Peel and brown onions and mix them with the meat; add tomatoes. Season and pour in broth. Cover and simmer until meat feels tender, about 45 minutes.

Stir flour into a small amount of water, and mix in with the stew together with crème fraîche or sour cream. Simmer for another 5 to 10 minutes. Season to taste. Serve with boiled potatotes. Makes 4 servings.

Crown Roast of Lamb with Onion and Apple Stuffing

Pork and Ham

Hawaiian Pork Chops

1 clove garlic, crushed	1 green pepper
Grated rind of half an orange	1 medium-sized onion
1 cup soy sauce	4 stalks white celery
¼ cup sherry or port	1 tablespoon oil
¼ teaspoon fresh ginger, grated	1 tablespoon butter
½ bay leaf, crushed	4 slices pineapple
Salt and pepper	1 cup chicken or veal stock
4 pork chops	Little paprika

Mix garlic, orange rind, soy sauce, sherry, ginger, bay leaf, salt, and pepper together; pour over chops. Leave at least 1 hour.

Remove seeds from pepper. Cut 4 rings; chop the rest. Chop onion and celery. Mix chopped vegetables together.

Remove chops from marinade; dry on paper towel. Heat oil; add butter. When foaming, put in chops; brown on both sides, about 2 to 3 minutes each side. Put into ovenproof dish with lid. Put pineapple slice and spoonful of vegetables on each chop.

Mix stock with remaining marinade; pour around chops. Cover; bake in preheated 350°F oven about 1 hour. If meat looks as if it is becoming dry, add a little more stock. During last 5 minutes put pepper rings on pineapple. Just before serving, dust each pineapple ring with paprika. Makes 4 servings.

Lamb with Vegetables

Normandy Pork Chops

4 pork loin chops	½ cup red wine or cider
2 tablespoons oil	1 teaspoon thyme, chopped
2 medium-sized onions, chopped	1 tablespoon parsley, chopped
1 clove garlic, crushed	1 bay leaf
5 medium-sized carrots	3 medium-sized cooking apples
2 celery stalks, cut into strips	1 cup mushrooms, quartered
1 tablespoon flour	1 tablespoon brown sugar
1 tablespoon tomato puree	
1½ cups stock (or water and cube)	

Brown chops on both sides in hot oil, about 2 minutes each side. Place in ovenproof dish with lid; keep warm.

Fry onions, garlic, carrots, and celery until golden brown. Stir in flour. Add tomato puree and stock; bring gently to boil, stirring constantly. Add wine and herbs. Pour over chops; replace lid. Bake in preheated 350°F oven 40 minutes.

Meanwhile, cut apples into rings. After 20 minutes add mushrooms to sauce; stir in well; lay apple rings in overlapping layer all over dish. Sprinkle with brown sugar; finish cooking with lid off dish. Makes 4 servings.

Pork with Cider

1½ pounds lean boneless pork, cut into 1-inch cubes	2 carrots, sliced
⅓ cup flour	1 small onion, sliced
⅓ cup vegetable oil	½ teaspoon rosemary
1½ cups apple cider or apple juice	1 bay leaf
	1 teaspoon salt
	½ teaspoon pepper

Thoroughly dredge pork with flour.

Heat oil in large frying pan until hot. Carefully add pork; cook until browned on all sides. Remove pork; drain on paper towels. Place in casserole.

Drain oil from pan. Pour in cider; heat and stir to remove browned pieces from pan.

Add carrots, onion, rosemary, bay leaf, salt, pepper, and hot cider to casserole; cover. Bake in 325°F oven 2 hours until meat is tender. Remove bay leaf. Makes 4 servings.

Pork Chops in Onion Sauce German-Style

4 **pork chops**	4 **small (or 2 medium)**
½ **teaspoon salt**	**onions, thinly sliced**
¼ **teaspoon pepper**	½ **cup beer**
1½ **teaspoons flour**	½ **cup hot beef broth**
1½ **tablespoons vegetable oil**	1 **teaspoon cornstarch**

Season pork with salt and pepper; coat with flour. Heat oil in heavy frying pan. Add chops; fry each side 3 minutes. Add onions; cook 5 minutes, turning chops once. Pour in beer and broth; cover. Simmer 15 minutes. Remove chops to preheated platter. Season sauce to taste.

Blend cornstarch with small amount cold water. Stir into sauce; cook until thick and bubbly. Pour over pork. Makes 4 servings.

Lamb Stew

Crown of Pork with Orange Rice

Crown of Pork with Orange Rice

2   (6 bone) pieces loin end of
    pork
Salt and pepper
4   tablespoons butter or
    margarine
1   cup celery, finely chopped
1   large onion, chopped
1   pound long-grain rice
2½ cups chicken stock or
    water and chicken stock
    cube

1   cup orange juice
½   cup raisins
1   level tablespoon orange
    rind, grated
Grapes and watercress for
    garnish

Ask your butcher to prepare meat for a crown. Form loins into a circle; sew them together with fine string and tie a double piece of string around to keep it in shape. Wrap ends of bones in foil. Sprinkle pork with salt and pepper and put in a roasting pan. Roast in 350°F oven for 30 minutes per pound plus 30 minutes over.

Make orange rice: Heat butter in a saucepan, and stir in celery, onion, rice, and 2 level teaspoons salt. Add stock and orange juice. Bring to a boil, stir, then cover pan tightly. Simmer rice gently for 15 minutes, or until tender and all liquid is absorbed. Stir in raisins and orange rind.

Put cooked pork on a serving plate and spoon orange rice into center. Remove foil from bones and garnish with grapes and watercress. Makes 12 servings.

Stuffed Pork Chops

Barbecue Sauce

1½ tablespoons oil
1 onion, chopped
1 clove garlic, crushed
1 teaspoon flour
1 small can tomatoes
1 cup brown stock
2 tablespoons vinegar
2 tablespoons Worcestershire sauce
1 tablespoon tomato chutney
1 tablespoon sugar
1 teaspoon lemon juice
1 tablespoon parsley and thyme, chopped
¼ teaspoon celery salt

Stuffing

1 onion, chopped
1 stalk celery, chopped
3 tablespoons butter
2 cups fresh bread crumbs
1 apple, chopped
4 tablespoons chopped parsley, thyme, and a little sage
Grated rind of ½ lemon
1 small egg, beaten
Few drops lemon juice
4 good-sized pork chops
2 to 3 tablespoons oil

Make barbecue sauce. Heat oil; cook onion and garlic, covered, 3 to 4 minutes to soften. Remove lid; brown slightly. Add flour; brown slightly. Add tomatoes and stock; bring to boil. Add all other ingredients; cook 15 minutes. Strain; set aside.

Make stuffing. Cook onion and celery in butter. Add to bread crumbs together with apple, herbs, and lemon rind. Bind mixture with egg and dash of lemon juice; if too dry, add a little milk or stock.

Make cut in center of side of each chop; be careful to make pocket without piercing top or bottom surface of meat. Push stuffing into pocket. Sew up or skewer slits in chops; pat dry. Brown both sides in a little hot oil; remove. Put into ovenproof dish. Spoon over a little barbecue sauce thinned with a little extra stock. Cook in preheated 350°F oven about 1 hour. Take out; remove threads or skewers. Serve with barbecue sauce. Makes 4 servings.

Pork Fillets

2 **pounds pork tenderloin**	1 **teaspoon salt**
1 **large apple**	¼ **teaspoon freshly ground**
2 **tablespoons almonds,**	**pepper**
chopped	¼ **cup olive oil**
1 **teaspoon sugar**	½ **cup dry red wine**
¼ **teaspoon cinnamon**	1 **cup stock**
¼ **teaspoon garlic powder**	

Slice tenderloin into 6 pieces.

Peel, core, and finely chop apple. Combine apple, almonds, sugar, and cinnamon; mix well.

Make horizontal slash in center of each tenderloin without cutting through. Stuff with apple filling. Press meat together; secure with metal clamps or skewers if necessary.

Combine garlic powder, salt, and pepper. Rub tenderloins with mixture. Heat oil in deep skillet; brown tenderloins on all sides. Add wine and stock; bring to boil. Reduce heat; simmer 1 hour, turning meat at 15-minute intervals. Makes 4 servings.

Japanese-Style Pork Loin

About 1 pound thick pork loin	2 **onions, minced**
	¼ **teaspoon black pepper**
Marinade	1 **clove garlic, crushed**
⅓ **cup oil**	1 **tablespoon vinegar**
2 **tablespoons not-too-salty**	5 **coriander seeds, crushed**
soy sauce	

Trim and cut loin into thick (1/2-inch) slices. Mix marinade ingredients together. Place pork in a greased pan and cover with marinade. Let stand in a cool place for about 24 hours.

Preheat oven to 400°F. Place plate with meat and the marinade in oven for about 20 minutes if pink and juicy meat is desired, somewhat longer if meat is to be well done. Baste several times with marinade while baking. Serve immediately with rice mixed with sliced mushrooms or raisins. Makes 4 servings.

Grilled Pork Delight

4 pieces thin belly pork or pork for frying	4 tablespoons cider or beer
⅔ cup cheese, grated	1 tomato, sliced, for garnish
½ level tablespoon prepared mustard	

Grill pork for 5 to 7 minutes on each side. Mix cheese, mustard, and cider or beer together in a bowl.

Spread topping equally over pork. Grill until brown. Garnish with a slice of tomato. Makes 4 servings.

Pork Roast with Cranberry Stuffing

Pork loin roast (8 rib chops), 6 to 7 pounds	1 cup cranberries, knife-chopped
Salt, pepper, poultry seasoning	1 small red appled (unpeeled), cored and diced (¾ cup)
1 cup boiling water	
1 beef bouillon cube	¼ cup celery, finely chopped
½ cup butter	¼ cup parsley, minced
1 (8-ounce) package herb-seasoned bread stuffing	1 large egg

Have butcher saw off backbone (chine) of roast. Place meat, rib-ends-up, on cutting board. Holding meaty side of the roast with 1 hand, starting 1 inch from one end of roast and ending 1 inch from other end, cut slit between meat and rib bones almost to bottom of roast. With fingers, pull meaty part slightly away from ribs to form pocket. Sprinkle inside of pocket and outside of roast with salt, pepper, and seasoning salt.

Into large skillet or medium saucepan, off heat, pour boiling water. Add bouillon cube; stir to dissolve. Add butter; over very low heat stir until melted. Remove from heat. Add bread stuffing, cranberries, apple, celery, and parsley; mix well.

Beat egg until thick and pale-colored; mix with stuffing. Spoon stuffing into pocket in roast; put any leftover stuffing into small baking dish. Roast pork on rack in shallow roasting pan in 350°F oven 35 minutes per pound.

About half an hour before roast is ready, put baking dish of extra stuffing in oven to heat. After roast has been removed to hot serving platter, pour off fat in roasting pan. Spoon some drippings over top of stuffing in roast and some over small baking dish of extra stuffing. Makes 6 servings.

Grilled Pork Delight

Muckalica

1	(1¾-pound) boneless loin of pork	4	tomatoes, chopped
2	tablespoons butter or margarine	4	pepperoni (fresh), cubed
2	green peppers, seeded and cubed	2	teaspoons soy sauce
		1¼	teaspoons salt
2	onions, chopped	½	teaspoon black pepper
		¾	cup sour cream
		1	onion, chopped

Trim meat by cutting away any extra pieces of fat, then cut meat into strips. Brown it well in the butter. Mix green peppers, onions, tomatoes, and pepperoni with the meat, decrease heat, and add soy sauce, salt, and pepper. Cover and simmer for about half an hour. If stew begins to look dry, add 1/4 cup water.

Serve with sour cream, chopped raw onion, and boiled rice. Makes 4 servings.

Barbecued Pork Ribs

1½ **cups catsup**	1 **tablespoon paprika**
¾ **cup chili sauce**	3¼ **teaspoons salt**
½ **cup vinegar**	1 **clove garlic, crushed**
6 **tablespoons Worcestershire sauce**	¼ **teaspoon hot-pepper sauce**
6 **tablespoons light brown sugar, firmly packed**	5 **pounds pork back ribs**
	½ **teaspoon pepper**
3 **tablespoons fresh lemon juice**	**Thin slices of onion and lemon (optional)**

Combine catsup, 1-1/2 cups water, chili sauce, vinegar, Worcestershire sauce, brown sugar, lemon juice, paprika, 2-1/4 teaspoons salt, garlic, and hot-pepper sauce in large saucepan. Heat to boiling; reduce heat. Simmer 30 to 45 minutes, until sauce is good basting consistency.

Cut meat into 3 to 4 rib portions. Sprinkle with 1 teaspoon salt and pepper. Put on rack in shallow baking pan. Bake at 450°F 30 minutes.

Remove from rack; drain off excess fat. Put ribs in baking pan meaty-side-down; brush with sauce. Reduce oven temperature to 300°F; bake 30 minutes. Turn ribs meaty-side-up; brush with sauce. Top each rib with an onion slice. Bake about 1 hour, brushing frequently with some remaining sauce, until ribs are tender and nicely browned. Add lemon slices to ribs during last half hour of baking. Serve remaining sauce on side. Makes 6 servings.

Barbecued Spareribs

3 **pounds spareribs**	1 **tablespoon Worcestershire sauce**
Salt and pepper	
1 **onion, finely chopped**	2 **level tablespoons brown sugar**
1 **tablespoon oil**	
1 **clove garlic (optional)**	**Watercress for garnish**
1 **cup tomato soup**	

Chop spareribs into separate ribs or ask the butcher to do this for you. Place in large saucepan with salted water to cover. Bring to a boil, cover pan, and simmer for 20 minutes.

Meanwhile, fry onion in oil in small saucepan until softened. Add garlic, tomato soup, Worcestershire sauce, brown sugar, and salt and pepper. Bring to a boil, stirring until sugar is dissolved. Cover pan and simmer for 10 minutes. Drain spareribs well.

Brush them with some of the sauce and cook over a moderately hot fire or in a broiler for 30 minutes, until golden and tender. Baste with the sauce and garnish with sprigs of watercress. Makes 4 servings.

Muckalica

Chinese Spareribs with Glazed Fresh Peppers

4 **pounds spareribs, cut into serving pieces**	⅓ **cup fresh lemon juice**
Salt	⅓ **cup soy sauce**
1 **pineapple**	2 **tablespoons butter**
⅔ **cup brown sugar, firmly packed**	½ **pound small fresh mushrooms**
3 **tablespoons cornstarch**	½ **cup fresh onion, chopped**
1 **teaspoon dry mustard**	1 **green sweet pepper, cut into squares**
1 **teaspoon ginger**	1 **red sweet pepper, cut into squares**
2 **cups fresh orange juice**	

Place spareribs, bone-side-down, in shallow baking pan; sprinkle with salt to taste. Bake in preheated 350°F oven 1 hour. Drain off excess fat.

Pare pineapple; cut in half lengthwise. Remove core; cut into cubes.

Combine brown sugar, 1/2 teaspoon salt, cornstarch, mustard, and ginger in medium-sized saucepan. Stir in orange and lemon juices and soy sauce; bring to boil. Cook until thickened, stirring constantly; remove from heat.

Melt butter in skillet. Add mushrooms; sauté 5 minutes, stirring frequently. Pour sauce over spareribs. Add onion, peppers, pineapple, and mushrooms. Bake 30 minutes; baste occasionally with sauce in pan. Makes 4 to 6 servings.

Pork Spareribs in Mexican Barbecue Sauce

Mexican Barbecue Sauce	2 **tablespoons chili powder**
1 **tablespoon olive oil**	2 **tablespoons sugar**
1 **medium onion, chopped**	¼ **cup vinegar**
1 **clove garlic, peeled, minced**	⅓ **cup olive oil**
1 **fresh chili pepper, stemmed, seeded, chopped**	¼ **cup beer**
½ **tablespoon salt**	4 **pounds pork spareribs (country-style)**
2 **large tomatoes, peeled, cut up**	

Make sauce. Heat oil in saucepan. Sauté onion until lightly browned. Add garlic, chili pepper, salt, and tomatoes; simmer until mixture thickens. Add chili powder, sugar, vinegar, olive oil, and beer; cook 8 minutes, stirring constantly.

Marinate spareribs in sauce several hours before grilling (if possible). Grill over hot charcoal or under broiler, basting periodically with sauce, until tender, well browned, and crusty. Pour extra sauce on the ribs before serving. Makes 6 to 8 servings.

Pork Stroganoff

1½ pounds shoulder of pork	**1⅔ cups strong beef broth**
4 onions	**2 tablespoons tomato paste**
Butter or margarine for frying	**1½ cups crème fraîche or sour**
Salt	**cream**
Pepper	**1 to 2 teaspoons soy sauce**

Cut meat into strips. Peel and slice onions. Brown meat in butter in a stew pot. Add salt and pepper. Add onions so that they also become brown.

Decrease heat and gradually add beef broth. Add tomato paste. Simmer meat and onions in gravy for about 25 minutes, or until meat is tender and thoroughly cooked. Cover pot when simmering meat.

Remove pot from heat and stir in crème fraîche. Bring to a boil and add soy sauce. This dish should have a rich and rather strong taste. Serve with rice. Makes 4 servings.

Barbecued Spareribs

Rolled Shoulder with Ham and Cheese

½ tablespoon butter
8 thin slices of lean pork shoulder, about 1 pound
¼ pound smoked ham, in thin slices
5 to 6 slices cheese

¾ teaspoon salt
¼ teaspoon black pepper
½ to ¾ teaspoon crushed sage (optional)
Tomato halves (optional)

Grease a roasting pan, placing a wide strip of butter along middle of pan. Place shoulder slices in middle of roasting pan. The slices should be placed in a row, slightly overlapping. Sprinkle with most of salt, pepper, and sage, if desired. Place ham and cheese on top.

Roll up meat, first from one side and then from the other, so that it becomes a long roll. Fasten with toothpicks; salt.

Bake in middle of a preheated 350°F oven until a toothpick goes easily through meat, about 45 minutes. Toward end of baking time, brush roll with a small amount of gravy and fat, which has collected in bottom of pan. If you wish, place tomato halves around meat when 15 minutes of baking time remains.

Cut roll up into slices and serve with boiled potatoes. Lightly salt and pepper tomatoes. Makes 4 servings.

Sweet-and-Sour Pork

1½ pounds lean pork, cut into 1-inch cubes
3 tablespoons soy sauce
3 tablespoons dry white wine
2 carrots, cut into thin strips
1 red sweet pepper, seeds removed and cut into thin rings
4 tablespoons olive oil
1 small slice fresh gingerroot, minced
½ cup onions, chopped
¼ pound fresh mushrooms, sliced

½ cup beef broth

Sweet-and-Sour Sauce
4 tablespoons catsup
¼ cup brown sugar
2 tablespoons soy sauce
3 tablespoons wine vinegar
2 tablespoons dry white wine
2 tablespoons cornstarch dissolved in ½ cup cold water

Place pork in shallow dish. Combine soy sauce and wine; pour over pork. Turn to coat all sides. Marinate about 20 to 30 minutes; stir frequently.

Cut carrots; set aside. Cut pepper into rings; set aside.

Heat 2 tablespoons oil in wok or skillet. Add gingerroot. Place pork in wok; stir-fry about 5 minutes. Remove pork; set aside. Add remaining oil to wok. Add carrots, pepper, onions, and mushrooms; stir-fry about 5 minutes

Pork Stroganoff

or until carrots and pepper are tender but still on crisp side. Add pork; stir-fry 5 minutes. Add broth; mix well.

Make sauce: Combine catsup, sugar, soy sauce, vinegar, and wine in saucepan; bring to boil. Add cornstarch dissolved in water to sauce. Cook over low heat, stirring constantly, until sauce has thickened. Add sauce to pork mixture; bring to boil. Reduce heat to low; cover wok. Cook 2 minutes. Serve with rice. Makes 4 servings.

Baked Pork Tenderloin

6	pork tenderloin steaks, 1-inch thick	1	cup onion, chopped
½	cup flour	1	clove garlic, minced
½	teaspoon salt	1	teaspoon ground ginger
¼	teaspoon pepper	1	(1-pound) can applesauce
2	tablespoons butter or oil	½	cup sauterne wine
		½	cup soy sauce

Flatten tenderloins slightly with cleaver; rub both sides with flour seasoned with salt and pepper. Brown in butter; transfer to oven-serving dish.

Pour off all but 2 tablespoons fat. Brown onion and garlic slightly. Stir in ginger.

Mix together applesauce, wine, and soy sauce; stir into onion mixture. Simmer 1 minute; pour over pork. Bake 1 hour in preheated 350°F oven. Makes 6 servings.

Frankfurters with Sauerkraut

1	(1-pound) can or bulk sauerkraut	**Freshly ground pepper to taste**
1	small onion, minced	1 medium-sized potato, grated
2	tablespoons bacon drippings	1 cup dry white wine (optional)
1½	teaspoons caraway seed (optional)	1 pound frankfurters

Place sauerkraut in colander. Rinse thoroughly with cold water; drain well.

Sauté onion in bacon drippings in large frying pan until transparent but not browned. Add sauerkraut, caraway seed, pepper, potato, and 1 cup water or dry white wine. Simmer, covered, 30 minutes or until liquid is absorbed.

Place frankfurters in steamer pan over hot water; steam 20 minutes. Turn sauerkraut into serving dish; arrange frankfurters on top. Makes 4 to 6 servings.

Rolled Shoulder with Ham and Cheese

Swedish-Style Pork

1¼ pounds lean, boned pork
    shoulder
1 tablespoon soy sauce
1 tablespoon oil
Black pepper
1½ pounds frozen potatoes,
    diced

3 tablespoons butter
1 onion, finely choppped
1½ teaspoons salt
4 raw egg yolks (optional)

Cut meat into small cubes and mix with soy sauce, oil, and black pepper. Sauté potatoes in 2 tablespoons of butter in large frying pan until soft and browned, about 10 minutes. Cook onion with potatoes for the last 3 to 4 minutes. Season with about 1 teaspoon salt.

Finally, sauté meat quickly in butter in a large, very hot pan—cook about 3 to 4 minutes. Season meat with 1/2 tcaspoon salt.

Serve meat and potatoes with a raw egg yolk, if desired. Makes 4 servings.

Baked Ham Party-Style

1 (6- to 8-pound) canned, cooked boned ham	¼ cup dried currants
1 unpeeled orange, thinly sliced	¼ teaspoon ground ginger
	1 tablespoon vinegar
Juice of 1 orange	1 tablespoon mustard
¼ cup anise-flavored liqueur	1 teaspoon Worcestershire sauce
½ cup brown sugar, packed	⅓ cup water

Heat ham in oven according to package directions. Set orange slices to side.

Blend remaining ingredients in blender. Heat in skillet; spoon over ham. Bake 1/2 hour or until glazed; baste with seasoning mixture. Arrange orange slices over ham; garnish with watercress. Makes 12 or more servings.

Baked Ham Slice

1 (1- to 1½-inch thick) center ham slice	Whole cloves
½ cup dark brown sugar	1 cup milk

Place ham in greased baking pan. Spread brown sugar on top; stud with cloves. Pour milk around sides. Bake in preheated 325°F oven 1 hour or until tender.

Pears (cored and halved lengthwise) cooked with ham during last 30 minutes make an attractive garnish. Makes 4 to 6 servings.

Country Ham with Redeye Gravy

6 ham slices, about ½-inch-thick	¾ cup strong black coffee

Fry ham slices 1 or 2 at a time, depending on skillet size, over medium-high heat. Fry 5 to 6 minutes per side. When done, remove to heated platter.

Pour off all but about 3 tablespoons fat in skillet. Brown remaining drippings; add coffee. Be sure to scrape up pan scrapings (these are the redeyes); bring to boil. Gravy can be spooned over ham or served separately. Serve with hot grits or biscuits to absorb gravy. Makes 6 servings.

Baked Glazed Ham

1 (2- to 3-pound) canned ham	½ cup cider or pineapple juice
2 tablespoons honey	1 tablespoon butter
Grated rind of 1 orange	1 small can pineapple rings
1 teaspoon dry mustard	Dusting of sugar
4 tablespoons brown sugar	6 to 8 canned sweet cherries

Scrape jelly off ham; reserve. Place in baking pan. Melt honey; spread over surface of ham. Mix orange rind, mustard, and brown sugar together; sprinkle over surface of meat. Pour cider over ham. Add jelly from ham; baste very gently over ham without disturbing sugar coating. Bake in preheated 400°F oven 30 minutes, basting after 15 minutes.

Melt butter in frying pan. Sprinkle pineapple slices with sugar; brown in butter on both sides. Serve around ham with cherries in center of each ring.

Use liquid from baking pan to make sauce; add water and squeeze of lemon if too sweet. Makes 4 to 6 servings.

Grilled Ham with Raisin and Cranberry Sauce

1½ to 2 pounds 1-inch-thick ham slices	1½ cups cranberry juice
Few cloves	½ cup orange juice
½ cup brown sugar	½ cup seeded or seedless raisins
2 tablespoons cornstarch	

Score fat edges of ham at intervals of about 2 inches; insert 2 or 3 cloves in fat.

Mix sugar and cornstarch smoothly with cranberry juice; put into pan. Add orange juice and raisins; bring to boil. Stir constantly until mixture thickens.

Put ham on grid over hot coals away from hottest part; cook about 15 minutes. Turn; brush liberally with glaze. Cook 10 minutes. Turn; brush other side. (Can be put on broiler rack in open pan 3 inches below unit. Allow 10 to 12 minutes on each side; brush with glaze as above.) Brush again just before serving; serve any remaining glaze with ham. Makes 4 or 5 servings.

Ham and Cottage Cheese Salad

Ham and Cottage Cheese Salad

1 cup cottage cheese	**4 slices ham**
Salt and pepper	**Few strips red or green pepper**
1 inch cucumber, chopped	**and cress for garnish**
Pinch of curry powder	

Combine cottage cheese, seasoning, cucumber, and curry powder. Divide between slices of ham and roll up. Arrange strips of red or green pepper across each ham roll and garnish with cress. Makes 4 servings.

Veal

Veal Birds

6 **thin slices veal breast**	**Salt and pepper**
¼ **cup soft white bread crumbs**	**Beaten egg**
	3 **tablespoons oil**
2 **tablespoons fat, chopped**	1 **onion, chopped**
1 **level tablespoon parsley, chopped**	2 **level tablespoons flour**
1 **level teaspoon dried thyme**	1½ **cups veal stock or water and chicken stock cube**
½ **level teaspoon lemon rind, grated**	**Chopped parsley for garnish**

Trim veal slices. If they are too thick, beat until thinner. Put bread crumbs into a bowl with fat, parsley, thyme, lemon rind, salt, and pepper. Mix in enough beaten egg to bind. Divide stuffing between the 6 slices of veal. Roll up each piece and secure with wooden cocktail sticks or thread.

Heat oil in a frying pan and fry rolls until browned all over. Put them in a casserole. Add onion to the pan and fry until softened. Stir in flour and cook, stirring, for 2 minutes. Gradually add stock and bring to a boil, stirring constantly. Season.

Pour sauce over veal rolls. Cover and cook in a 325°F oven for 1-1/4 hours. Remove skewers or thread and serve garnished with chopped parsley. Makes 6 servings.

Veal Birds

Veal with Artichokes

1 **clove garlic**	1 **cup canned tomatoes**
1 **tablespoon vegetable oil**	¼ **cup sherry**
1 **pound veal round, cut into**	¼ **teaspoon oregano**
bite-sized pieces, pounded	1 **(10-ounce) package frozen**
½ **teaspoon salt**	**artichoke hearts**
⅛ **teaspoon pepper**	

In large frying pan, sauté garlic in hot oil. Remove garlic; discard.

Season veal with salt and pepper; brown in oil. Add tomatoes, sherry, and oregano; mix well. Add artichoke hearts; cover. Simmer 1 hour or until meat is tender. Makes 4 servings.

Blanquette de Veau

2 **pounds veal from shoulder**	1 **bay leaf**
or breast	**Sprig of thyme (or ¼ teaspoon**
4 **tablespoons butter**	**dried thyme)**
1 **onion, quartered**	12 **baby or pickling onions**
3 or 4 **medium-sized carrots**	12 **button mushrooms**
1 **tablespoon flour**	1 **large or 2 small egg yolks**
2 **cups chicken or veal stock**	1 **cup cream**
Parsley stems	**Squeeze of lemon**

Cut veal into cubes about 1-1/4 inches square. Put into pan with enough cold water to cover and a little salt. Bring slowly to boil; cook 5 minutes. Skim scum from surface; drain meat. Wash well with cold water; dry.

Melt 3 tablespoons butter. Cook veal cubes slowly with quartered onion and carrots; shake frequently. Do not let them brown at all. Stir in flour. Add stock, parsley, bay leaf, and thyme; bring to boil. Place in pre-heated 350°F oven or simmer on stove 1 to 1-1/2 hours until veal is tender.

Meanwhile, peel baby onions; cook in salted water 10 to 15 minutes; drain. Melt remaining butter. Cook mushrooms a few minutes; add to onions.

Remove veal from stove; place meat in dish. Add carrots, baby onions, and mushrooms. Strain cooking liquid; boil to reduce quantity slightly. Remove from heat; cool slightly.

Beat egg yolks with cream; add a little hot sauce. Strain mixture gradually into sauce. Add lemon juice. Do not boil under any circumstances after this point. Pour over meat and vegetables. Serve at once with mashed or riced potatoes or plain boiled rice. Makes 4 to 6 servings.

Hungarian Veal Chops

1½ tablespoons paprika	1 small onion or shallot,
1 teaspoon salt	finely chopped
Pepper	½ cup white wine
4 veal chops	½ cup cream
2 to 3 tablespoons butter	Chopped parsley

Mix 2 teaspoons paprika with salt and pepper. Sprinkle on both sides of chops; rub in gently.

Melt 2 tablespoons butter in frying pan; cook chops about 2 minutes on each side, until well browned. Remove; keep warm. Add onion to frying pan; cook gently until tender. Add remaining paprika; cover. Cook 1 or 2 minutes. Return chops to pan; add few drops wine. Bake in preheated 350°F oven about 20 minutes. Place on serving dish to keep warm.

Pour wine into pan; reduce by cooking a few minutes. Stir in cream; simmer. Stir in remaining butter and pour over chops. Sprinkle top with parsley. Serve with plain boiled noodles. Makes 4 servings.

Veal Cordon Bleu

1½ to 1¾ pounds veal cutlets,	¾ cup fine dry bread crumbs
cut into 6 thin pieces	1 can condensed cream of
6 thin slices boiled ham	mushroom soup
3 slices Swiss cheese	Paprika
1 egg, slightly beaten	
2 tablespoons plus ½ cup	
milk	

Pound each veal piece to 1/8 inch thick; top each with ham slice. Cut each cheese slice into 4 strips; place 2 on each ham slice. Roll meat around cheese; secure with wooden picks.

Mix egg and 2 tablespoons milk; dip rolls in egg, then in crumbs. Place seam-side-down in 13 × 9 × 2-inch baking dish.

Combine soup, wine, and 1/2 cup milk; heat to bubbling. Pour around rolls; cover with foil. Bake in preheated 350°F oven 1 hour or until meat is tender; uncover. Sprinkle with a little paprika; bake 10 minutes or until crumbs are browned. Makes 6 servings.

Veal with Cheese

4 (3-ounce) veal slices	**Fresh bread crumbs**
2 slices processed cheese	**Oil for frying**
Salt and Pepper	**Lemon slices and parsley for**
Flour	**garnish**
1 egg, beaten	

Place veal between 2 pieces of waxed paper and beat until very thin. Cut cheese slices in half. Fold each piece of veal around a piece of cheese to make a neat parcel. Season flour and coat the veal. Dip veal in egg, then coat in bread crumbs. Press coating on firmly.

Heat a little oil in a frying pan and fry veal parcels until golden, turning once. Garnish with lemon slices and sprigs of parsley. Serve immediately. Makes 4 servings.

Veal Breast with Herb Stuffing

Herb Stuffing

3 strips bacon	**⅓ cup sour cream**
1 medium-sized onion	**½ teaspoon salt**
1 (4-ounce) can mushroom pieces	**¼ teaspoon pepper**
¼ cup fresh parsley, chopped	**Veal**
1 tablespoon fresh dill, chopped	**3 to 4 pounds boned veal breast or leg**
1 teaspoon dried tarragon leaves	**½ teaspoon salt**
1 teaspoon dried basil leaves	**¼ teaspoon pepper**
½ pound lean ground beef	**1 tablespoon vegetable oil**
½ cup dried bread crumbs	**2 cups hot beef broth**
3 eggs, beaten	**2 tablespoons cornstarch**
	½ cup sour cream

Prepare stuffing. Dice bacon and onion. Cook bacon in frying pan until partially cooked. Add onion; cook 5 minutes.

Drain and chop mushrooms; add to frying pan. Cook 5 minutes; remove from heat. Let cool; transfer to mixing bowl. Add herbs, beef, crumbs, eggs, and sour cream; mix thoroughly. Season with salt and pepper.

With sharp knife, cut pocket in veal; fill with stuffing. Close opening with toothpicks. (Tie with string if necessary.) Rub outside with salt and pepper.

Heat oil in Dutch oven or heavy saucepan; place meat in pan. Bake in preheated 350°F oven about 1-1/2 hours; baste occasionally with beef broth. When done, place meat on preheated platter.

Veal with Cheese

Pour rest of beef broth into Dutch oven; scrape brown particles from bottom. Bring to simmer. Thoroughly blend cornstarch with sour cream; add to pan drippings, stirring. Cook and stir until thick and bubbly.

Slice veal breast. Serve sauce separately. Makes 6 servings.

Braised Veal Cutlets in Sherry

3 veal cutlets, cut into serving pieces	½ cup sherry
Flour	¼ teaspoon salt
Salt	2 tablespoons parsley, chopped
Pepper	4 thin slices boiled ham
2 tablespoons butter	4 thin slices Swiss or Romano cheese
½ cup consommé	
½ cup water	

Dust cutlets with flour, salt, and pepper; sauté lightly in butter. Cover with consommé, water, and wine. Sprinkle with 1/4 teaspoon salt and parsley; cover. Bake in preheated 350°F oven 1 hour; uncover.

Place slice of ham and cheese on each cutlet; return to oven until cheese melts. Serve at once. Makes 4 to 6 servings.

Veal with Mushrooms

2 pounds boneless, thinly sliced veal cutlet or fillet	3 tablespoons butter
½ cup flour	1 pound mushrooms, sliced
1 teaspoon salt	6 tablespoons wine
¼ teaspoon pepper	2 tablespoons lemon juice
2 tablespoons vegetable oil	Lemon slices for garnish

Gently pound veal into very thin pieces. Mix flour, salt, and pepper; lightly flour veal. Melt oil and butter in 10-inch frying pan; sauté veal until golden brown, about 3 minutes each side. Remove; keep warm.

Add mushrooms to frying pan; cook several minutes. Add wine and lemon juice; boil rapidly to reduce sauce slightly. Pour over veal; garnish with lemon slices. Makes 6 servings.

Veal Piccata

4 pieces scallopine of veal	1 clove garlic, crushed
2 tablespoons flour	¼ cup dry vermouth
4 tablespoons corn-oil margarine	1 tablespoon lemon juice
	½ lemon, sliced

Pound veal with wooden mallet until very thin (1/8-inch). Dredge lightly in flour; shake off excess.

Melt 3 tablespoons margarine in skillet. Place garlic in skillet until golden brown; discard.

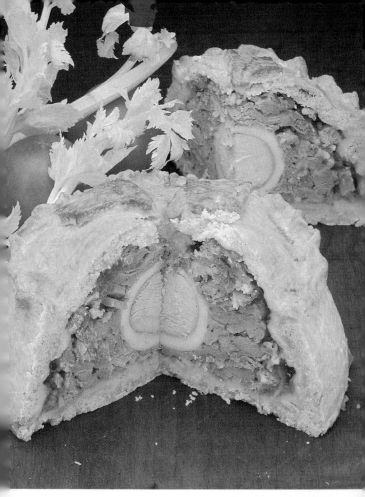

Veal, Ham, and Egg Pie

Place veal in skillet; cook quickly, just until brown, about 1 to 2 minutes each side. Remove to serving dish.

Add remaining margarine, wine, and lemon juice to pan; simmer 3 minutes, scraping bottom of pan to loosen drippings. Pour over veal. Garnish with lemon slices. Makes 4 servings.

Veal with Rice and Sour Cream

1½ pounds veal, cut into small pieces	2 tablespoons parsley, minced
2 tablespoons oil	1 teaspoon paprika
1 medium-sized onion, chopped	3 cups beef broth
1 clove garlic, minced	1 cup uncooked rice
1 medium-sized green pepper, chopped	1 cup sour cream
	Salt and pepper to taste

Brown veal in oil. Add onion, garlic, and green pepper; cook a few minutes. Add parsley, paprika, and broth; simmer, covered, 15 minutes. Add rice; stir. Cover; cook 15 minutes.

Slowly stir in sour cream. Season to taste; cover. Cook 15 minutes. Serve hot. Makes 4 to 6 servings.

Greek-Style Veal with Vegetables

2 tablespoons flour	**Flour**
3 tablespoons Kafaloteri or Parmesan cheese	6 tablespoons butter
½ teaspoon salt	1 eggplant, 1½ pounds
¼ teaspoon pepper	2 tablespoons olive oil
¼ teaspoon nutmeg	4 tomatoes, peeled and quartered
1 egg, beaten	Salt and pepper
½ cup milk	½ teaspoon rosemary
1 pound thinly sliced leg of veal, cut into serving-size pieces	Juice of 1 lemon
	2 tablespoons parsley, chopped

Combine flour, cheese, salt, pepper, and nutmeg. Add egg and milk; beat until well blended.

Wipe veal with damp cloth; dredge in flour. Melt 3 tablespoons butter in skillet until it sizzles. Dip veal in flour and egg batter; fry in butter until golden. Turn; fry other side. Remove to platter; keep warm.

Trim stem and cap from eggplant. Leaving skin on, slice 1/4 inch thick; pour boiling water over. Let stand few minutes; drain.

Heat oil in medium-sized skillet; add eggplant, tomatoes, salt and pepper to taste, and rosemary. Steam 10 minutes or until eggplant is tender; stir several times.

Arrange vegetables in serving dish. Arrange veal on top of vegetables. Melt remaining butter in pan in which veal was cooked until it foams. Add lemon juice and parsley; pour over veal. Makes 4 servings.

Milanese Veal Rolls

1½ **pounds rump roast of veal or veal cutlet**	1 **clove garlic, minced**
Salt and pepper	1 **(16-ounce) can Italian-style peeled tomatoes**
Ground sage	½ **cup white wine**
4 **slices prosciutto**	**Salt and pepper**
8 **thin slices mozzarella cheese**	8 **thin strips mozzarella cheese**
3 **tablespoons olive oil**	**Parsley sprigs**
1 **small onion, chopped**	

Pound meat with mallet to 1/8 inch thick; sprinkle with salt, pepper, and a little sage. Cut into 8 rectangular pieces.

Cut prosciutto slices in half. Top veal pieces with piece of ham and slice of mozzarella. Roll jelly-roll fashion; tie with string.

Heat oil in large skillet; sauté veal rolls until browned. Remove from pan. Add onion and garlic to pan; sauté until tender.

Break up tomatoes with fork; add to skillet, with wine, salt, and pepper; mix well. Add veal rolls; cover. Simmer 1-1/2 hours or until tender. Top with mozzarella strips; cover. Melt cheese. Serve on bed of hot cooked spaghetti; top with sauce and garnish with parsley sprigs. Makes 4 servings.

Veal Scallopino Parmagiano

4 **thin veal scallops (slices from leg of veal)**	3 to 4 **tablespoons Parmesan cheese, grated**
1 **large egg**	3 **tablespoons butter**
½ **tablespoon oil**	**Juice of ½ lemon**
3 **tablespoons flour**	1 **tablespoon parsley, finely chopped**
Salt and pepper	
½ **teaspoon powdered garlic**	

Beat scallops between waxed paper. Mix egg with oil; beat. Add seasoning and garlic to flour; mix with cheese. Brush scallops with egg mixture; press into cheese and flour until completely coated.

Melt butter; fry scallops until golden brown, about 5 to 6 minutes each side. Place on warm serving dish; keep hot.

Add lemon juice to butter in pan; reheat. Pour over scallops just before serving; decorate with parsley. Makes 4 servings.

Veal, Ham, and Egg Pie

Pastry
1¼ cups flour
½ level teaspoon salt
6 tablespoons water
¼ pound lard
Milk for glazing

Filling
¾ pound veal, finely
   chopped

¼ pound bacon
1 level teaspoon grated
   lemon rind
¼ level teaspoon mixed dried
   herbs
Salt and pepper
1 hard-boiled egg
Beaten egg
½ cup veal and ham stock
1 level teaspoon gelatin

Sift flour and salt. Boil water and lard in a pan and mix quickly into the flour. Knead until smooth. Remove 1/3 of the dough and keep hot. Quickly mold the large piece of dough around a 2-pound jar and then leave for 10 minutes.

Make filling: Chop veal and bacon finely. Mix veal and bacon with lemon rind and herbs; season well with salt and pepper.

Fill the pastry case with 1/3 of the filling, add hard-boiled egg, and pack in the remaining filling. Flatten the remaining pastry to a round the size of the pie. Brush edges of pie with beaten egg and cover with the lid. Press edges together and make a hole in the center (large enough to pour the stock through eventually). Brush pie with beaten egg.

Bake in a 375°F oven for 1-1/4 to 1-1/2 hours or until pastry is golden and meat cooked. If pastry becomes too browned, cover it with foil. Allow to cool.

Dissolve gelatin in the stock in a bowl over hot water, then pour it through the hole in the top of the pie when cool. Refrigerate pie until cold and the stock jellied. Serve cold. Makes 6 servings.

Veal Marengo

1 pound veal (lean breast or
   stew meat), cubed
2 tablespoons vegetable oil
1 medium-sized onion,
   chopped
¼ pound fresh mushrooms,
   sliced
1 medium-sized carrot,
   sliced
1 tablespoon tomato paste

½ teaspoon salt
⅛ teaspoon pepper
1 bay leaf ·
1 teaspoon dried thyme
½ cup hot water
½ cup white wine
¼ cup plain yogurt
1 tomato (garnish)
Parsley (garnish)

In large frying pan, brown meat in hot oil several minutes. Remove meat; keep warm.

Add onion, mushrooms, and carrot to pan drippings; cook 5 minutes. Stir in tomato paste; season with salt and pepper. Add bay leaf and thyme; pour in water and wine. Return meat to pan; cover. Simmer about 30 minutes; cool slightly. Gradually add yogurt; reheat over low heat, if necessary, but do not simmer. Remove bay leaf; adjust seasonings. Serve on preheated platter; garnish with tomato sections and parsley. Makes 4 servings.

Veal Schnitzel with Spinach and Sherry Sauce

Veal Steaks with Lemon and Curry

1 **pound veal cutlets, thinly sliced**	2 **tablespoons evaporated milk**
½ **teaspoon salt**	2 **tablespoons tomato paste**
¼ **teaspoon pepper**	1 **lemon, juiced**
¾ **teaspoon curry powder**	10 **sprigs parsley, chopped**
3 **tablespoons vegetable oil**	2 **tablespoons cognac or brandy**
2 **onions, diced**	

Season veal with salt, pepper, and 1/2 teaspoon curry. Heat oil; brown veal slices on both sides. Remove meat and reserve.

Add onions; sauté until softened. Add evaporated milk and tomato paste. Cook until bubbly. Add lemon juice, rest of curry, and chopped parsley. Return veal slices to sauce. Add cognac or brandy; heat through. Serve on warmed platter. Makes 4 servings.

Wiener Schnitzel

4 **large (6-ounce) thin veal scallops**	4 **slices lemon**
2 to 3 **tablespoons flour**	4 **olives**
Salt and pepper	4 **anchovies**
1 **egg**	1 **hard-boiled egg, chopped**
Vegetable oil	2 **teaspoons capers, chopped**
5 to 6 **tablespoons dried white bread crumbs**	2 **teaspoons paprika**
2 to 3 **tablespoons butter**	2 **tablespoons parsley, chopped**

Beat scallops between pieces of waxed paper until wafer-thin. Toss in seasoned flour until completely coated; shake to remove excess.

Beat egg with few drips of oil and some salt. Brush each scallop with this; toss in crumbs. (A paper bag is a good container for this.)

Melt butter in frying pan. When foaming, cook veal 3 to 4 minutes each side, until golden brown and crisp. Place on hot dish; garnish top of each scallop with 1 lemon slice. Place an olive in center; curl an anchovy fillet around olive. Surround with portion of egg white, capers, and paprika. Sprinkle all over with parsley. Decorate with sieved egg yolk, if desired. Serve at once, with remaining butter from frying pan as sauce. (Extra butter can be added.) Makes 4 servings.

Veal Schnitzel with Spinach and Sherry Sauce

1 **(10-ounce) box frozen spinach**	2 **veal cutlets**
½ **pound asparagus tips**	2 **teaspoons butter**
½ **teaspoon salt**	1½ **teaspoons soy sauce**
⅛ **teaspoon pepper**	1 **teaspoon arrowroot, potato flour, or cornstarch**
⅛ **teaspoon garlic powder**	2 **tablespoons sherry**
¼ **teaspoon crushed basil**	

Cook spinach in its own juice over medium heat. When tender, drain and reserve liquid. Cook asparagus tips in 1/2 cup boiling salted water for 4 to 5 minutes. Drain and combine liquid with spinach broth.

Combine spices; rub half of them into cutlets and season spinach with the rest.

Heat a skillet, preferably a nonstick one; add butter and sauté cutlets, 1 to 2 minutes on each side. Place cutlets on a heated platter along with asparagus and spinach. Cover with foil and keep warm while making sauce.

Boil vegetable broth until it measures approximately 2/3 cup. Add soy sauce. Mix thickener with sherry and add it to broth, stirring constantly. Bring to a boil and season with salt and pepper. Pour sauce around meat and serve immediately. Makes 2 servings.

EQUIVALENT MEASURES

dash = 2 or 3 drops
pinch = amount that can be held
between ends of thumb &
forefinger
1 tablespoon = 3 teaspoons
¼ cup = 4 tablespoons
⅓ cup = 5 tablespoons + 1 teaspoon
½ cup = 8 tablespoons
1 cup = 16 tablespoons
1 pint = 2 cups
1 quart = 4 cups
1 gallon = 4 quarts
1 peck = 8 quarts
1 bushel = 4 pecks
1 pound = 16 ounces

KITCHEN METRIC

measurements you will encounter
most often in recipes are: centimeter
(cm), milliliter (ml), gram (g),
kilogram (kg)

cup equivalents (volume):

¼ cup = 60 ml
⅓ cup = 85 ml
½ cup = 125 ml
⅔ cup = 170 ml
¾ cup = 180 ml
1 cup = 250 ml
1¼ cups = 310 ml
1½ cups = 375 ml
2 cups = 500 ml
3 cups = 750 ml
5 cups = 1250 ml

spoonful equivalents (volume):

⅛ teaspoon = .5 ml
⅓ teaspoon = 1.5 ml
½ teaspoon = 3 ml
¾ teaspoon = 4 ml
1 teaspoon = 5 ml
1 tablespoon = 15 ml
2 tablespoons = 30 ml
3 tablespoons = 45 ml

pan sizes (linear & volume):

1 inch = 2.5 cm
8-inch square = 20-cm square
9 × 13 × 1½-inch = 20 × 33 × 4-cm
10 × 6 × 2-inch = 25 × 15 × 5-cm
13 × 9 × 2-inch = 33 × 23 × 5-cm
7½ × 12 × 1½-inch = 18 × 30 × 4-cm
(above are baking dishes, pans)
9 × 5 × 3-inch = 23 × 13 × 8-cm
(loaf pan)
10-inch = 25 cm   12-inch = 30-cm
(skillets)
1-quart = 1-liter   2-quart = 2-liter
(baking dishes, by volume)
5- to 6-cup = 1.5-liter
(ring mold)

weight (meat amounts;
can & package sizes):

1	ounce	= 28 g
½	pound	= 225 g
¾	pound	= 340 g
1	pound	= 450 g
1½	pounds	= 675 g
2	pounds	= 900 g
3	pounds	= 1.4 kg (in recipes, amounts of meat above 2 pounds will generally be stated in kilograms)
10	ounces	= 280 g (most frozen vegetables)
10½	ounces	= 294 g (most condensed soups)
15	ounces	= 425 g (common can size)
16	ounces	= 450 g (common can size)
1	pound, 24 ounces	= 850 g (can size)

OVEN TEMPERATURES

275°F = 135°C
300°F = 149°C
325°F = 165°C
350°F = 175°C
375°F = 190°C
400°F = 205°C
425°F = 218°C
450°F = 230°C
500°F = 260°C

Note that Celsius temperatures are
sometimes rounded off to the nearest
reading ending in 0 or 5; the Celsius
thermometer is the same as
Centigrade, a term no longer used.

Index